BLOODY B
HISTO

CW00644632

COVENTRY

BLOODY BRITISH HISTORY

HISTORY

COVENTRY

DAVID McGRORY

The phoenix rises.

First published in 2013

The History Press
The Mill, Brimscombe Port
Stroud, Gloucestershire, GL5 2QG
www.thehistorypress.co.uk

© David McGrory, 2013

The right of David McGrory to be identified as the Author
of this work has been asserted in accordance with the
Copyrights, Designs and Patents Act 1988.

British Library Cataloguing in Publication Data.
A catalogue record for this book is available from the British Library.

ISBN 978 0 7524 9344 2

Typesetting and origination by The History Press
Printed in Great Britain

CONTENTS

ACKNOWLEDGEMENTS

THE SOURCES FOR this book have been gathered over a number of years. However, I would like to particularly thank Rob Orland; Mark Twissell; John Hewitson; Nicola Norman; Coventry Local Studies; John Ashby; Tony Rose and the Coventry Police Museum; Colin Walker; Derek Lee; Holy Trinity Church; the Sealed Knot; Warwick Archives; and the British Library.

Note: All images are from the collection of the author or the publisher unless otherwise credited.

A BRIEF WORD ON
THE BLITZ

COVENTRY HAS A long and sometimes bloody past.

Its origins lie in the mists of time, but there is evidence of Roman activity, including ditches and tracks in the centre. What the Romans were doing here we do not know, but they left statues, coins, brooches and pottery behind them. At the nearby Lunt, outside of Coventry, lay a fort, home to Roman cavalry who at one time trained captured Iceni horses after the Boudican Revolt.

During its early history Coventry was sacked by the Danes. Then, during the medieval period, the city grew to prominence because of its dealings with wool and cloth and became particularly known for its long-lasting, blue-dyed cloth, called Coventry True Blue. During this period the city grew in status, becoming the fourth largest city in England. It was also during this period that St Osburga's grew into the massive cathedral and priory of St Mary. The city has welcomed many monarchs, including Henry VI (who based his royal court here for three years during the Wars of the Roses). The city's strong wall held out against

Yorkist forces, as it later did against Charles I during the Civil War in 1642.

After the war, Coventry took on more the appearance of a town than a city, crammed full of timbered houses. The principal trades of the city up until the nineteenth century were mainly cloth and silk ribbon weaving. Later, however, after these industries collapsed, things turned more mechanical with the introduction of cycle, and then motor-car manufacture. The mechanisation of the city's industries led to it being a main centre for war production in both the First and Second World Wars.

The Second World War, of course, held major consequences for the city when it became the target for Nazi bombing from June 1940. Many people living in Coventry today lost family members and friends during those terrible years. For this reason, I have decided not to discuss these events in detail in this volume, a decision which I hope my readers will understand. However, it was certainly a time we should look back on and remember for the suffering and the strength of the people of Coventry. Indeed, it is almost impossible to overstate the devastation caused to Coventry during the Second World War, or the bravery of its inhabitants during those dark times.

After Coventry-built Whitley bombers attacked Munich, the birthplace of the Nazi party, Hitler ordered retribution – and Coventry was chosen as the target, codenamed Corn.

Operation Moonlight Sonata began from airfields in France on the evening of 14 November 1940. Beams that intersected over Coventry led the Luftwaffe pathfinders, the first of 500 here, and they began to lay a firestorm. The first of 30,000 incendiaries dropped that night. The city burned and the heavy bombers that followed continually dropped their devastating loads for eleven long hours.

Some squadrons were given factories as targets, but most were simply instructed to bomb the heart out of the old city. Stories still persist that Churchill sacrificed Coventry to protect the Enigma Code, even though these stories have been proved to be untrue for over forty years. But plays and tales still keep the story alive, and many now believe it. The air-raid sirens screamed the all-clear at 6.16 a.m. on the following morning. The people of Coventry walked out into the devastation: their city would never be the same again.

During the previous night the Luftwaffe had unloaded 500 tons of high explosives, 30,000 incendiaries

and 50 land and oil mines. Amongst the ruined city, 554 people lay dead and 865 injured. This was the worst of forty-one actual raids on the city, though the following April raids were nearly as bad (lasting eight and nine hours respectively).

Despite their suffering, the people of Coventry proved resilient and took, time after time, what the Nazis threw at them. By the end of the war over 1,200 citizens were dead, but still the city's spirit was unshaken. The results of this devastation have shaped the city ever since, and Coventry today still lives with the consequences of those dark times.

Beyond those dark nights lay another Coventry, a Coventry of 1,000 years, where Vikings burned a nunnery, knights attacked a castle, bishops were bad and religious martyrs were murdered by the Church. Plague raged through old Coventry, as did floods. The city was placed under siege by a King himself – more than once, too. Elections, meanwhile, weren't the sedate affairs they are now: they were traditionally a time in which men with big sticks fought to control the vote. Amazingly, these wars were usually led by the Corporation itself.

In the pages that follow lie that city beyond the Blitz, beyond the phoenix rising. Old Coventry, a city full of real, 'bloody' brilliant history. Enjoy.

David McGrory, 2013

AD 1002

DEATH TO THE DANES!

ON 13 NOVEMBER 1002 Coventry took part in one of early history's bloodiest events – the St Brice's Day Massacre. Coventry at this time was a small settlement in the kingdom of Mercia, scattered around the nunnery of St Osburga. St Osburg's, as it became known, probably stood off present Priory Row. The buildings from this earliest incarnation were built over by the later priory. By St Brice's Day, this house was long established: during excavation work in 2000 a curved wall, possibly of the apse, was discovered on the site of the later priory which had green mortar. Beneath this wall was a burial dating back to around AD 690, proof that this area had been occupied for more than 300 years by the eleventh century.

Much of this history was violent: we are informed that in the days of this nunnery, in AD 829, Ecgbryth, King of Wessex, overcame the Mercian kingdom. In AD 910 the land of the Mercians was again under assault, when it was 'ravaged' by the Danes. We do not know whether this attack affected the small settlement that

would become Coventry. However, there was one obvious result of the raids: this time the conquering Danes settled in Coventry and its surrounds – and indeed some Danish names remain, such as Biggin, part of Stoke, which comes from a Danish

A late Anglo-Saxon door jamb, probably from St Osburg's, which was dug up early in the last century in Palmer Lane.

name meaning house, and Keresley and Allesley, both Danish names for settlements.

Danish communities, and Danish attacks, had by this time reached such numbers that they began to threaten the safety of the realm. The *Anglo-Saxon Chronicle* records that the King, Æthelred II ('the Unready'), was told that unless he removed the Danish menace they 'would faithlessly take his life, and then all his councillors, and possess his kingdom afterwards.' He therefore 'ordered slain all the Danish men who were in England.'

On the night of St Brice's Day, 13 November, according to a message passed in secret through the realm, every Danish man, woman and child in the country was slaughtered. This command was carried out with

A Victorian engraving of the St Brice's Day Massacre, when possibly all the Danes in England were killed by the English.

ruthless efficiency. The King's Royal Charter in Oxford, where weapon-scarred skeletons from the period have been found, describes the massacre in that city:

> ... all the Danes who had sprung up in this island, sprouting like cockle amongst the wheat, were to be destroyed by a most just extermination, and thus this decree was to be put into effect even as far as death. Those Danes who dwelt in the afore-mentioned town, striving to escape death, entered this sanctuary of Christ [St Frideswide's], having broken by force the doors and bolts, and resolved to make refuge and defence for themselves therein against the people of the town and the suburbs; but when all the people in pursuit strove, forced by necessity, to drive them out, and could not, they set fire to the planks and burnt, as it seems, this church with its ornaments and its books.

Centuries later, in 1565, Queen Elizabeth arrived in Coventry. The city recorder gave a speech, and the St Brice's Day Massacre was the first topic on the agenda: 'after the arrival of the Daynes who misrablye afflicted the people of the Realme,' the recorder announced, 'the inhabitants of this Citie with ther neighboures utterly overthrewe them in the laste conflicte with the Saxons.'

The memory of this massacre in Coventry was commemorated for centuries yearly on St Brice's Day, when the men of Coventry would perform a re-enactment of the massacre which they called the 'Hoc Tuesday Play'

This they performed to Elizabeth herself during her next visit, this time to Kenilworth, in 1574. During this knockabout performance Elizabeth is said to have 'much laughed', an ironic finale to the memory of a massacre!

This wasn't the city's last tussle with the Danes, however, for in the year 1016 the *Anglo-Saxon Chronicle* informs us that, 'In this year came Cnut with his host, and with him ealdorman Eadric, and crossed into Warwickshire, and harried and burnt and slew all they found.' This army was led through the county by one who knew it well: Eadric Streona, also known as 'Eadric the Traitor' or 'Grasper'. The fifteenth-century priest and antiquarian John Rous, who had access to now-lost documents, described how this army destroyed a Saxon stronghold at Stoneleigh. He also wrote, 'even the abbey of Nuns at Coventry is destroyed, of which in times past the Virgin St Osburg was the Abbess.'

Though this army obviously burned and sacked the original St Osburg's, some of her relics remained – for her skull, and some of her bones, were re-housed in new reliquaries and survived up until the Dissolution in the sixteenth century. King Canute later added another major relic: the arm of St Augustine of Hippo. Such a gift, it was said, 'would gain him many friends and prayers.' A Viking iron axe, decorated with bronze strips of this

Canute with his Queen, Emma, gifting a large cross to a church. Canute spent many years trying to make up for the devastation he had previously caused in England.

period and of the type used in warfare, was unearthed in Coventry by John Shelton after the war and still remains in the museum's collection. Canute became King and later, in 1027, he vowed to make up for the destruction he had brought down on so many religious houses. The sixteenth-century antiquarian John Leland, quoting ancient sources, states that Coventry Priory was formerly the place where 'Kynge Canute the Dane made [a] howse of nunes. Leofrike, Erle of the Marches, turnyd it in Kyng Edward the Confessor's days into a howse of monkes.' By all accounts Canute ruled well and agreed to rule under one God and to avoid heathen practices.

'GLITTERING IN ARMS'

Civil War Conquests in Coventry

COVENTRY SEEMS TO disappear from history after the convent became a monastery – until, that is, the building of a motte-and-bailey castle here by the 4th Earl of Chester, Ranulf Gernon (1129-1153). Ranulf is described in a contemporary source as, 'a consummate warrior, glittering in arms.' Gernon, a French nobleman and a supporter of Matilda during the Baron's War, was a legend of the era, particularly famous for his valour at the Battle of Lincoln, where his army captured King Stephen.

One source describes the capture of Stephen thus:

Knights skirmish during the twelfth century in what was effectively the first Civil War. This time, however, no one fought for the people, but for Stephen and Matilda.

[Stephen] remained on the battlefield, fighting on foot, though assaulted by multitudes, which he repelled with incredible valour ... His battle-axe was broken by the force and frequency of the blows he dealt around him. He then drew his sword and for a considerable time continued to defend himself, until his sword flying into fragments, and he being at the same instant struck down with a stone, William de Keynes, one of the soldiers of the earl of Gloucester [Gernon's father-in-law, who led the reserve], rushed in upon him, and seizing hold of his helmet, set his sword against his throat, and threatened him with instant death if he did not yield himself prisoner.

Gernon's greatest enemy was Robert Marmion II of Tamworth, a supporter of Stephen. The pair's enmity swiftly followed them to Warwickshire.

Walter of Newburgh wrote that Marmion 'had no match for boldness, cunning and fierceness.' In 1142 Marmion came to Coventry and expelled the monks from the monastery – 'locking out the servants of God and introducing to it the hire

THE HISTORY OF THE CASTLE

Ranulf's title was inherited by his six-year-old son Hugh Kevelioc. Kevelioc received his inheritance when he was eighteen years old, in 1162, and rebuilt the castle in stone. In his boundary charter we get the first mention of Broadgate, 'the broad gate of my castle'. Within the wall of this castle stood the chapel of St Michael in the Bailey, later to become the old cathedral. In 1173, now twenty-nine, Hugh Kevelioc joined a rebellion against Henry II. Henry sent a force to besiege Coventry Castle led by Richard de Lucy. Hugh was taken prisoner and was deprived of his land. The castle may have sustained considerable damage during this attack.

During the period when the fortress was in the hands of Kevelioc's son, Ranulf Blondeville, it began to fall from use. In a charter dated between 1199 and 1204 Blondeville forbids his constables from bringing the burghers into the castle to plead their causes.

After this date the castle disappears from history, leaving us with just stones, rubble, ditches and tales. Names also survived such as the Stiltyard (tilt yard), *fossatum castelli*, the castle ditch, and Castelbachous (castle bake house). The bake house was by St Mary's Hall, which stands in the former site of the castle and was constructed out of the old castle's stone.

A Norman stone castle keep. Although Coventry's first castle was a wooden motte-and-bailey structure, it was later replaced by a stone keep.

hands of the Devil' – and fortified it, placing the castle under siege. His plan was to cut off the food supply, starving the occupants into surrender. This siege is said to have continued until 8 September 1143, when the earl's men broke loose and a bloody fight ensued outside the fortified monastery. Sir William Dugdale, Warwickshire's most noted seventeenth-century historian, describes the surprising result of this battle:

[Marmion] fortified the church with the buildings belonging thereunto, making deep trenches in the fields adjacent, which he so covered, that they could not be seen. ... But it so happened, that as he sallied out with some forces upon the Earl of Chester's drawing near, and not remembering where those places had been digged, he fell with his horse into one of them himself, and by that means, being surprised by a common soldier, had his head presently cut off.

Other versions have it that the fall broke Marmion's thigh bone. While struggling on the ground, it was said,

SKELETAL MONKS

Skeletons were unearthed in Coventry in August 1936:

> In the process of underpinning the walls of Blue Coat School as part of the work necessary in connection with the development of Trinity Street, excavations have brought to light a number of skeletons. The bones were found huddled against an old stone wall which had lain buried for hundreds of years. Their position suggested that the bodies of which they had once formed the framework had been buried together, while cleavages of the skulls of several of them appeared to have been caused during lifetime and not since the burial of the bodies. (*Coventry Herald*)

Apparently the teeth showed most of the skulls to be of young men, and local antiquarian John Bailey Shelton suggested that they had died in battles around the city. It was thought that the skeletons were about 700 years old, giving a suggested death date of around AD 1200 or before. This would put the men into the period of the sieges involving Coventry Castle, during the Baron's War. As we know, when Robert Marmion put Coventry Castle under siege in 1142-3 it is said he turned out the monks from

A medieval skeleton being unearthed in Coventry in 1932 on the site of the present Central Hall.

the monastery and fortified it. There is of course a possibility that the monks never left the precinct of their house. However, if these skeletons are not those of the monks, it is probable that they were the skeletons of Civil War soldiers.

---

he was dispatched by a cobbler with a knife.

Later on in the war, in 1145, Ranulf Gernon changed sides. He defected from Matilda's cause, and switched to Stephen's. However, he quickly fell out with the King and was captured, and forced to swear on holy relics that he would give up all of his castles and never again resist the King. Stephen therefore took possession of Ranulf's castle at Coventry. It was not an

oath that Gernon was to keep: *Gesta Stephani*, 'The Life of Stephen', tells us that in 1146, on being released from his chains, Gernon 'burst into a blind fury of rebellion, scarcely discriminating between friend or foe'. He gathered a force and 'reduced the country to a desert':

> The earl also established a strong post in the face of the castle of Coventry in which the Royalists had taken refuge.

SIEGE WEAPONS IN POOL MEADOW

The attacks on Coventry by Danish armies and by the forces of the King were not to be the last. The year 1395 saw Sir William Bagot of Baginton Castle, with 100 armed men, trying – and failing – to breach two of the city gates. This appears to have been an organised rising against the mayor and an attempt to take control of the city. Other attacks seemed to have been made on the city, for in the past four trebuchet balls have been unearthed, the last two in the 1960s below Pool Meadow. These were cast over the city walls by massive trebuchets, huge and devastating siege weapons that flung huge balls of rock to smash the walls and cause terror beyond.

... Whereupon the King, marching there at the head of a gallant force, threw a convoy of provisions into the garrison, which were much needed, though he had frequent skirmishes with the Earl, who lay in wait for him. ... In these, some of the King's troops were captured, and others driven to flight, and the King himself received a slight wound. ... But shortly afterwards recovering his strength, he had an engagement with the Earl, in which he took many prisoners, and some of the enemy were wounded, and the Earl himself flying shamefully and scarcely escaping with his life, his fortified post was taken and destroyed.

Ranulf did later regain Coventry, but his victory was short-lived as he died under mysterious circumstances, just six months later, in December 1153 – according to many sources, he drank wine poisoned by one of Stephen's stoutest allies, William Peverel the Younger, a knight whom Gernon had captured with King Stephen all those years before.

CRUSHED BY A STONE FROM HEAVEN

The Horrible Death of a Coventry Monk

THE NEARBY PRIORY of St Mary was the scene of a number of bloody incidents in Coventry's history, one of which involved the sudden and unexpected death, in 1185, of the Bishop of Coventry, one Gerard le Pucelle.

No images survive of Hugh de Nonant, but this early seal suggests how his clothes may have looked. This is Richard Peche, Bishop of Coventry from 1161 to 1182.

The bishop, like others before him, was laid to rest in the Chapter House – but rumours that he had been poisoned persisted. Another bishop who followed him may have had knowledge of the event – or may even have arranged it. Known as Hugh de Nonant, this bishop was once an advisor to King Richard I, and had previously held the position of sheriff of Staffordshire. He acquired the See not by election but by cash, helping to fund Richard's Crusade. From the beginning the monks hated him, but perhaps not as much as he hated them. Nonant was a noted monk-hater: he was once heard to say 'to perdition with monks! If I had my will, not one should be left in England.' Coventry Priory was in trouble!

One of Nonant's first acts on attaining the Bishopric was to ignore papal decree and move his chair away from Coventry to Lichfield, home of secular canons rather than of monks. He thereafter bore down on the monks of Coventry, cutting their food supply and sacking their quarters. Their personal possessions were taken into his treasury. He removed the prior's

A meeting in a Chapter House. The Chapter House at Coventry, as elsewhere, contained the remains of deceased bishops and priors. It was thought their presence would add to any debates – and their remains could, if necessary, be sworn on.

power, making himself all-powerful in the region. This, not surprisingly, led to trouble. The men of the priory may have been under Holy Orders, but they were not to be trifled with.

Richard of Devizes described what happened next:

> On a certain day when the bishop was superintending the workpeople at Coventry ... [he] said, 'I call my clerks gods, and my monks devils.'
>
> And thereupon wagging his finger ... towards his clerks, who stood about ... he continued, 'I say ye are gods, and ye are all children of the Highest ... But ye monks shall perish like devils ... ye shall fall away into hell, because ye are devils upon earth. Verily, if I should have to officiate for a dead monk, which I should loath to do, so I should commend his soul to the devil, not to God.

COVENTRY IS FULL OF ASSASSINS!

Other notable assassination attempts are connected with Coventry. Robert of Gloucester wrote, in the following century:

> A council had been held until late one winter's eve at the Royal Manor of Woodstock, to consider and remedy the growing troubles of the State, but as deepening shadows grew apace, the King [Henry III, 1216-72] left the Hall, tired and weary, for the rest of his chamber.
>
> But with his mind filled with anxious cares sleep forsook him, and luckily it was so, for a grating noise, as of someone endeavouring to undo the fastenings of the window, aroused him ... so pulling aside the arras he beheld a tall figure unfastening the lattice. Noiselessly he called his attendants from an adjoining room, who, after a struggle, succeeded in effecting a capture, and when the prisoner was brought before the King he said he was a priest named Ribbaud, and was connected with a northern monastery.

Ribbaud confessed that his intention was to kill the King. At his trial he was condemned to be taken to Coventry and there, in Broadgate, before the people, to be 'torne by wild horses, and drawn thro' the streets till life leave bodie.' Afterwards, when life was extinct, Ribbaud's corpse was hanged, drawn and quartered. His parts were displayed in cities throughout the realm to show 'traitors that would be' what was waiting for them.

The minute he finished these words a stone fell, or was dropped, from the tower above, missing him by inches but bursting out the brains of the monk next to him.

What happened next suggests that this accident had in fact been a deliberate attempt to assassinate the unpopular prelate. During a synod held in the priory church an argument broke out between Nonant and the monks. This synod ended – according to the bishop – with a group of monks actually attacking him before the high altar and smashing his head open with a crucifix. Nonant had them charged with contaminating the church by spilling his blood and the monks were expelled entirely from the priory and replaced with canons. Prior Moyses went into exile in Rome – where all but one of the monks with him died of want and starvation – and the order was scattered. It took them eight years to return. Meanwhile, Nonant – now allied to King John – grew more powerful. However, on Richard's return he was cast from office, though he eventually regained it by paying 5,000 marks.

When Nonant died, in 1198, many bishops gathered around his death bed to hear his dying confession. It was reported that they stood in shocked silence, 'hearing of such a wicked life'. Many reports have it, however, that the bishop repented of his treatment of the Coventry monks on his death bed, and that his last request was that he should be dressed so that he could die in the habit of a monk of the same order.

AD 1398

TRIAL BY COMBAT

OVENTRY'S GOSFORD GREEN is a particularly important historic site. Here British history was changed forever by an event which, in the end, didn't even take place.

It began with a casual meeting near London of the favourites of King Richard II, Thomas Mowbray, 1st Duke of Norfolk and Constable of Calais, and Henry Bolingbroke, Duke of Hereford. Each man accused the other of treason. Richard had both men arrested and brought before Parliament where Hereford then accused Norfolk of the murder of his dear uncle, the Duke of Gloucester. This was a killing Norfolk had actually performed as the King's agent. As it was decided by Parliament that the charges could not be proved, the matter was put into the hands of God – and trial by combat was declared.

At a second select meeting at Windsor it was decided that Hereford and Norfolk should meet on St Lambert's Day, Monday, 17 September 1398, on Gosford Green, outside the city wall of Coventry, to prove their words before God

and the people. The combat was proclaimed throughout the realm and into France and both men made preparations. Hereford had a new suit of armour created by the armourers of the Duke of Milan, while Norfolk's armour was made by German master armourers. On the Sunday before the fight Hereford came to the King, who was lodged in a tower belonging to Sir William Bagot about a quarter of a mile outside the city. The following day Norfolk also took leave of the King.

Thousands came to Coventry on the designated day to witness the trial. Norfolk spent the night at his castle at Caludon and Hereford stayed

A brass of Sir William Bagot from Baginton Church. Bagot, who once attacked Coventry, hosted the King and Norfolk. Little remains of his once large castle.

at Baginton Castle, home of Sir William. It is said that he changed into his armour in a tent near the lists, while Norfolk changed in a large house surrounded by a wood between Gosford Gate and the Green. The Duke of Aumale and the Duke of Surrey took control of the lists with men carrying pikes. Holinshed describes what followed:

> With a great company of men apparelled in silk sendall, embroidered with silver, both richly and curiously; every man had a tipped staff to keep the field in order. About the hour of prime [6 a.m.] came to the barriers of the lists the Duke of Hereford, mounted on a white courser, barded with green and blue velvet, embroidered sumptuously with swans and antelopes of goldsmith's work, armed at all points.

King Richard II visited Coventry more than once. In September 1385 he visited with his Queen, Anne of Bohemia, and laid the foundation stone of the Carthusian Charterhouse on the London Road. He was back for the combat in 1398 and again for a last visit – when he passed through Coventry as a prisoner.

The constable and marshall approached Hereford and demanded aloud the reason he had come to Coventry. He answered: 'I am Henry of Lancaster, Duke of Hereford. I have come here to do my endeavour against Thomas Mowbray, Duke of Norfolk, as a traitor, untrue to God, the King, his realm and me.' He then unsheathed his sword, held it before him and swore his quarrel was true and just. He re-sheathed it, entered the list, dismounted and sat in a great chair covered in green velvet.

Next King Richard entered, accompanied by all the peers of the realm, and took his richly decorated seat on the great dais, followed by the peers. The King was accompanied by over 10,000 men, 'in armour,

lest some fray or tumult might arise amongst his nobles.' A proclamation was made that no man should enter the lists on pain of death. This proclamation concluded with, 'Behold Henry of Lancaster, Duke of Hereford, appellant has entered the royal list to do his endeavour against Thomas Mowbray, Duke of Norfolk, defendant, upon pain to be found false and recreant.'

Holinshed reported that: 'The Duke of Norfolk hovered on horseback at the entry to the lists, his horse being barded with crimson velvet, embroidered richly with lions of silver and mulberry trees.'

He made his oath that his quarrel was just, and entered the field calling aloud, 'God aid him that hath the right.' He dismounted and sat in a chair at the other end of the lists. The lord marshall then checked both men's lances and returned them, and they were ordered to horse. The Duke of Hereford leapt onto his horse and as the trumpet called spurred it forward, lance ready, thundering towards his adversary. Norfolk had just began to spur forward when suddenly the King threw down his sceptre and the heralds rushed forward shouting, 'Ho! Ho!'

Instantly Hereford, shocked by events, reined his horse back, while Norfolk practically stumbled to a halt. Called to hold, the men struggled with their horses as they circled around in an agitated state. They were asked to give over their lances and to retake their seats, which they did for two hours, as Richard took council.

Eventually the heralds called for silence as the King's secretary Sir John Bushy read out the results of their deliberation. The combat was cancelled. However, within fifteen days Henry, Duke of Hereford, was ordered to leave the realm, not to return for ten years, unless ordered by the King, on pain of death. He was, however, given a yearly income of £2,000. This was small comfort, for the secretary had one more announcement for him: his estates were to be confiscated.

Thomas Mowbray, the Duke of Norfolk, and Henry Bolingbroke, the Duke of Hereford, prepare for combat in this excellent nineteenth-century engraving showing Coventry in the background.

As for Mowbray, who was thought to have 'sown sedition in the land' by his words, he was to leave the realm and never return, upon pain of death. He was given a yearly income of £1,000, and his property was confiscated. Both were then summoned to stand before the King and swear an oath that they would not continue the argument. This they did and then, along with the thousands that gathered, the men left the lists, stunned by the day's events.

The Duke of Norfolk left the realm and is said to have died of melancholy in Venice – though some sources say it was of 'pestilence', or plague. Henry Bolingbroke, the Duke of Hereford, a much more popular man, left via Kent, watched by 40,000 Londoners in 'tears and lamentations ... The wonder it was to see what number of people ran after him, in every towne and street.'

Henry Bolingbroke, King Henry IV of England.

Richard was campaigning in Ireland, Henry landed in England with an army to claim the English throne through the line of Edward III, his grandfather. Richard returned to England, but was forced to abdicate. Henry Bolingbroke, Duke of Hereford, became King Henry IV. So began the Lancastrian reign. Henry's image can be seen in the King's Window in St Mary's Hall.

The last time King Richard II passed through Coventry he was a prisoner. He was placed in Pontefract Castle where, in 1400, he was murdered, probably on the order of Henry, the man he had exiled at Coventry. Henry held a Parliament, called the *Parliamentum Indoctorum* – the Unlearned Parliament – because lawyers were prohibited from entering, at the Great Chamber of Coventry Priory in 1404. He died in 1413 in the Jerusalem Chamber, Westminster Abbey – fulfilling a prophecy that he would die in Jerusalem.

His exile was reduced by his father's pleading by four years. Any love or loyalty he felt towards the King had by then collapsed – especially in 1399, when his father, John of Gaunt, died and Richard confiscated his vast estate, Henry's birthright, and announced his exile was for life. In June 1399, while

THE COVENTRY MARTYRS

NO ONE SHOULD be murdered for their faith: everyone has the right to believe what they wish. In the past, of course, this wasn't always so, and many suffered – mainly when the country veered from one faith to the next.

Coventry in these days was a hotbed of religious reform, and from the fourteenth century it was already a well-established home to Lollardism. Lollardism had been developed from the preaching of John Wycliffe, the vicar of Lutterworth, who besides translating the scriptures into English was to carry his voice around England, proclaiming, 'The Bishop of Rome hath no jurisdiction in this realm of England.'

Large numbers of his followers were first noted in Coventry in 1423, where a crowd gathered for five days in the Little Park to listen to the preaching of John Grace. This was stopped by the Church and city leaders, and Grace was thrown into Coventry Gaol. In 1485 nine men were examined by the Bishop of Coventry for claiming that St Peter was the head of the Church, and that the Virgin was to be worshipped; the nature of the Mass was also discussed. After being interrogated the men refused to recant and were cast into the gaol.

Three years later, in 1488, Margery Goit was accused of denying the

John Wycliffe, rector of nearby Lutterworth church, not only defied the Pope – he also questioned the Catholic faith and published religious tracts, and a Bible, in English.

doctrine of the transubstantiation (that the bread eaten and wine drunk during Mass becomes the actual flesh and blood of Christ as it is consumed). She was forced to walk through the market place bearing a heavy bundle of faggots as a warning – next time, went the warning, they would be used to burn her on. In 1510, the year of Henry VIII's visit, ten Lollards accused of heresy were also forced to carry heavy bundles of faggots in penance before the people. All save one recanted – Joan Ward was burnt at the stake in the Park Hollows, a large shallow sandpit in the Little Park.

In 1519, Geoffrey Blyth, Bishop of Coventry, sent seven people to their deaths: Alice Smith, *née* Lansdail, a widow; Thomas Lansdail, her brother-in-law, a hosier; Horsea Hawkins, a skinner; Thomas Wrexham (or Wrigsham), a glover; Robert Hockett and Thomas Bond, shoemakers; and Robert Silksby. All were to be 'purified by the Church' – i.e. burned alive. All were to be tied to a stake in the Little Park for the heinous crime of saying the Lord's Prayer and Ten Commandments in English, instead of Latin.

Alice was initially discharged. However, she was not to escape for long. As the earliest 1576 edition of the *Acts and Monuments* has it:

And because it was in the euenyng being somewhat darke, as she should go home, the foresayd Simon Mourton the Somner offered him selfe to go home with her. Now as he was leadyng her by the arme, and heard the rattelyng of a scrole within her sleue: yea (sayeth he) What haue ye here? And so tooke

it from her, and espyed that it was the Lordes prayer, the Articles of the faith, & x. Commaundemetes in Englishe. Which when the wretched Somner vnderstode, ah serrha (said he) come, as good now as an other tyme, and so brought her backe agayne to the Byshop, where she was immediatly condemned for hauing the Lordes prayer in Englishe.

She was condemned to burn with the others. Robert Silksby, meanwhile, escaped. However, two years later he was rearrested and suffered the same fate – he was burned in the Hollows. The children of these martyrs, who had been taught the Lord's Prayer and the Ten Commandments in English, were taken to the monks of Grey Friars. Here they were examined by Friar Stafford. The friar warned them, 'vppon payne of suffering such death as their fathers, [that they] should in no wise to meddle any more with the lords prayer, the Crede, and commaundements in English. &c.' That is, if they didn't want to suffer the same fate as their parents they should stick to Latin.

Henry VIII later, when wishing to remarry, split from Rome and England became Protestant; when his daughter Mary was crowned in 1553, however, it soon became apparent that she wished to return to the Catholic faith. 'Bloody' Mary's reputation spread throughout England as innocent Protestants burned.

In Coventry the first to suffer was Lawrence Saunders, who was ordained in 1547 and became rector of All Hallows in Bread Street,

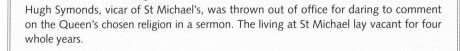

Hugh Symonds, vicar of St Michael's, was thrown out of office for daring to comment on the Queen's chosen religion in a sermon. The living at St Michael lay vacant for four whole years.

London. He preached in Northampton against Popish doctrine and called the Church a 'papist serpent'. That afternoon he returned to his church and was arrested. He was brought before the Bishop of London, and was imprisoned for fifteen months for treason and heresy. More than a year later he was brought forward again and was offered mercy if he would give up his 'abominable heresies and false doctrine'. Saunders repeated that what he did was a matter of his own conscience and that he only taught the 'purity of the Word'. At the end of this interview Bishop Bonner produced a document attacking the Catholic Church and with no evidence accused Saunders of writing it. He then pronounced him a heretic, returned him to prison and had him excommunicated and 'degraded' by the Bishop of London. This done, Saunders said to the bishop, 'I thank God I am not of your Church'. The following day he was delivered up to the Queen's Guard and brought to Coventry.

Coventry was probably picked because of its association with Lollardism and the fact that Saunders was well known here. On arrival he was spotted by a poor shoemaker who used to make his shoes, who said, 'O my good master, God strengthen and comfort you.' Saunders replied, 'Good shoemaker, pray for me, for I am the unfittest man for this high office, that was ever appointed to it; but my God and dear Father is able to make me strong enough.' He was placed amongst the rest of the prisoners in the common gaol and spent the night in prayer.

Of the morning of 8 February 1555, as Foxe noted (in text from a later addition, for ease of reading):

...he was led to the place of execution in the park, without the city. He went in an old gown and a shirt, and barefooted, and he often fell flat on the ground and prayed. When he had come nigh to the place, the officer who was appointed to see the execution done said that he was one of those who marred the Queen's realm with false doctrine and heresy, 'Wherefore thou hast deserved death, and yet if thou wilt revoke thine heresies, the Queen hath pardoned thee; if not, yonder fire is prepared for thee.'

'It is not I,' Saunders replied:

...nor my fellow preachers of God's truth, that hath hurt the Queen's realm, but it is yourself, and such as you are, who hath always resisted God's holy word. It is you who hath

Lawrence Saunders meets his shocking end in this sixteenth-century engraving from Foxe's Book of Martyrs.

and do mar the Queen's realm. I do hold no heresies but the doctrine of God, the blessed Gospel of Christ; that I hold, that I believe, that I have taught, and that I will never revoke.

With that his tormentor cried, 'Away with him!'

Saunders continued his last walk. When he reached the stake he fell to the ground and prayed. He clasped the stake to him and kissed it, saying, 'Welcome the cross of Christ, welcome everlasting life.' He was chained, and 'the fire being put to him, full sweetly he slept in the Lord.'

Foxe's fine words do not fully represent the truly horrific death Saunders suffered at the hands of the Church, for it was noted at the time that the wood used to 'cleanse' him was green, meaning it burned slowly, with lots of smoke, putting him through unbelievable agonies.

THE PERSECUTION OF THE GLOVERS

The next innocent to suffer was Robert Glover, who was educated at Eton and Oxford. In the beginning of 1555, according to Foxe, the Bishop of Coventry ordered the mayor and officers of the city to arrest John Glover of Mancetter on suspicion of heresy. The mayor instead sent a private warning to Glover before the officers were dispatched, and John escaped with a brother, William, just before they arrived. However, 'when John could not be found, one of the officers going in the upper chamber, found Robert, the other brother lying in his bed, and sick of a severe disease; he instead was immediately brought before the sheriff.'

Realising this was the wrong man, the sheriff wished to release him but an officer persuaded him to wait for the bishop to take the decision.

Eleven days later Glover was called to answer charges – despite the fact that they had nothing to charge him with and held no official document for his arrest. The summoner would have none of it. Glover himself wrote about what followed:

The second day after the bishop's coming to Coventry, Master Warren came to the Guildhall, and commanded the chief gaoler to carry me to the bishop. I laid to Master Warren's charge the cruel seeking of my death; and when he would have excused himself, I told him he could not wipe his hands so; as he was guilty of my blood before God as though he had murdered

LETTERS FROM A PRISON CELL

—⊶⊷—

While awaiting his fate, Robert wrote to his wife, Mary, from Coventry Gaol:

I thank you most heartily, most loving wife, for your letters sent to me in my imprisonment. I read them with tears, I say for joy and gladness, that God hath wrought in you so merciful a work … Wherefore, I thought it my bounden duty, both to God and man … to set aside all fear, perils and dangers … and persuaded all that professed God's word, manfully to persist in the defence of the same, not with sword and violence but with suffering and loss of life, rather than to defile themselves again with the whorish abomination of the Roman Antichrist.

—⊶⊷—

me with his own hands ... And so he departed from me saying, 'I need not to fear if I would be of his belief.' ... When he came before the bishop in one Denton's house he began by protesting that he was my bishop, and willed me to submit myself. I said to him, 'I am not come to accuse myself; what have you to lay my charge?'

The bishop asked Glover if he was learned, to which he replied, 'smally learned'. The chancellor informed the bishop he was in fact a Master of Arts. Then the bishop laid a charge against Glover that he had failed to attend church service. Glover replied that he would not attend their church as long as their Mass was used. Then Glover asked the bishop to show him one 'jot' in the scripture for the defence of the Mass.

The interrogation continued and the chancellor accused Glover of being arrogant. He then sent him back to the common gaol, with the bishop then ordering Glover's removal to Lichfield. Glover continues in his letter to his wife: 'Certain serjeants and constables of Coventry being appointed to convey

us to Lichfield, to be delivered there to one Jepcot, the chancellor's man, we were commanded to mount on horseback about eleven or twelve o'clock on Friday, being market day, that we might be more gazed and wondered at; and to kindle people's hearts against us.'

He was again interrogated in Lichfield and, despite his sickness, was kept alone in a small cell with nothing but a New Testament and a prayer book in Latin. Refusing to return to the bishop's church, Robert Glover was declared a heretic and ordered to be returned to Coventry for execution.

Robert spent his last night in Coventry Gaol in the company of Austen Berner of Southam, who ministered to him and promised that God would be with him. The following day, 19 September 1555, Glover was led to the stake, during which journey he spotted Berner amongst the crowds, clapped his hands joyfully, and cried to him, 'Austen, he [the Lord] is come, he is come!'

He did not die alone that day, for in the fire with him was Cornelius Bungay, a capper, who maintained

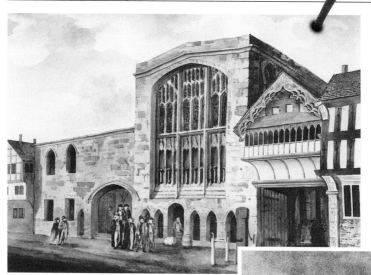

Above *St Mary's Guildhall, the best and oldest in England. Glover himself tells us that Master Warren came to see the gaoler in the hall. We don't know if the hall at the time was temporarily used as a prison for Glover.*

Right *The* Book of Martyrs *shows Glover and Cornelias Bungay being 'clensed' by the Church.*

that priests had no power to forgive sins and that the bread and wine used in the sacrament remain bread and wine throughout. He argued that the Pope was not the head of the earthly Church. Not surprisingly, given the climate of the times, he was condemned for teaching heretical doctrines in Coventry and Lichfield.

The Glover family's persecution did not stop after Robert's execution, for the Bishop of Coventry and Lichfield ordered a new search for John Glover. Again John escaped – but this time his wife Agnes was taken. John hid in the woods nearby, where he soon became ill and died. His body was later discovered and buried in the churchyard. Hearing of this, the chancellor ordered that it be exhumed and thrown into the road. However, when he was informed that the body had been in the ground for six weeks and smelled terribly he ordered its reburial – but not before Glover, from the church's pulpit, was cursed as a heretic and pronounced a damned soul. Twelve months later his bones were unearthed again and cast into the common highway, so 'that carts and horses may tread upon them'. When the last brother, William, died, the curate of his church, not wishing to bury him, contacted the bishop. This was his reply:

> Understanding that one Glover, a heretic is dead ... a rebel against our holy faith and religion ... and never required to be reconciled to our mother holy church ... I thought it good ... to command the curate ... that he should not be buried with a Christian man's burial ... nor speak to have him buried in holy ground ... but I do charge and command that he is not buried either in the church, or within the limits of the churchyard ... I charge those that brought the body to the place, to carry it away again ... or they will answer at their peril. At Ecclesch, this 6th September, AD 1555.
> By your Ordinary,
> RADULPH [of] COVENTRY AND LICHFIELD

By now William Glover's body was beginning to smell. He was lashed up to two horses and dragged into a broom field, where he was buried.

CARELESS AND PALMER

There were two other Coventry men who fell in the name of religion, though not in Coventry itself. John Careless, a weaver, was arrested in Coventry in November 1554. He was described by his inquisitor as 'one of the pleasantest Protestants I have ever met.' Careless spent two years in Coventry Gaol, his wife and children with him. He was well liked by the gaolers and was allowed to leave the gaol, on his word, to act in the pageants. After two years he was sent to London and there found guilty of heresy. While there he wrote a letter: 'My friends in Coventry have put the Council in remembrance of me, not six days ago saying, "I am more worthy to be burned than any that was burned yet".' However, Careless escaped the fire, not by any kindness of the Church but because he developed a sickness and died in prison. The Church took his final dignity from him nonetheless – they had him buried in a common dunghill.

A nineteenth-century engraving showing Glover's body being dragged from the churchyard by order of the bishop.

John Careless, loved by many Coventrians, spent over two years in Coventry Gaol before meeting his end.

The second man was Jocelyn Palmer, son of Coventry's mayor, Roger Palmer. He was also a Fellow of Magdalen College, Oxford. Palmer spoke Latin and Greek and, unlike the previous victims, he was originally Catholic. However, after witnessing the burning of Ridley and Latimer he had changed his faith. For his new-found beliefs he lost his Fellowship and was thrown out of Oxford. He then obtained a post as schoolmaster in Reading but was found out and dismissed. Jocelyn Palmer was made to answer for his beliefs, and was 'cleansed' at the stake in July 1557.

In 1854 the keeper of Quinton Park, as it was then, wrote:

The Martyrs Memorial was unveiled in 1910 as a permanent reminder of the cost of religious intolerance. It no longer stands on its original site, but now stands a few yards away on an island at the bottom of Little Park Street.

> I was digging in the Park Hollows; and when I had dug down about six feet from the surface I came to some very black soil, altogether different from that which I had dug through. I also found some charred or burnt wood, some cinders, and pieces of bright coal. I also found a number of bones, and pieces of silk, which might have been part of a dress, close by the bones.

A runic cross was set up in 1910 to commemorate Coventry's martyrs. The story of the martyrs is particularly close to my own heart, as my Cambridge-educated great-uncle (eleven times over), Francis Kett, was burned as a heretic in the ditch of Norwich Castle on 14 January 1587. It was said he went to the stake dressed in sackcloth and cried nothing but, 'Blessed be God ... and so continued until the fire consumed his nether parts, and until he was stifled by the smoke.'

AD 1642-1662

'ASSAULT THE SAID CITTIE'

Civil War Comes to Coventry

IN 1642 A census was taken of the city, and 9,500 souls were found to be living here. Of those, apparently only 400 Royalists could be identified.

As is well known, the formal declaration of the Civil War was the raising of the royal standard at Nottingham in August 1642. However, minor skirmishes happened months before this when people began to take sides. In May, Charles, testing the water, summoned the mayor and sheriffs to attend him in Leicester. As they were leaving, however, a huge crowd gathered to stop the delegation leaving the city. Two days later it was ordered that all inhabitants of the city, 'being of abilitie', should arm themselves. The local leaders began to ready themselves for conflict.

One such pair were Spencer Compton, Lord Northampton, the city recorder, and Lord Brooke of Warwick Castle, lord lieutenant of Warwick. They had great animosity towards one another: Brooke publically announced that Northampton should be 'hanged from the castle wall', food for crows and kites. In June 1642 a group, probably prompted by Northampton,

smashed up Brooke's family chapel in Warwick. Groups in Coventry began to pick and wear colours, and everyone began to fear their neighbour. Despite all this the city fathers hadn't totally committed themselves, for it was ordered that if the King did visit a purse of 200 gold pieces should be presented to him.

About a week before the standard was raised a royal army of about 6,000 to 10,000 soldiers, led by the King himself, approached Coventry. The *Iter Carolinum*, a diary of one of the King's personal attendants, informs us that the King was in Leicester on 18 August. The next day he moved south into Warwickshire, arriving at Stoneleigh Abbey, the home of the Leigh family, on the same day. While there the King received information from Northampton, saying that he would hold the city and its powder and weapon magazines for him. Four hundred armed men arrived in the city from Birmingham and Northampton and tried to build up Royalist resistance in the Bull Inn in Smithford Street. Things, however, began to get decidedly sticky and they were forced to flee

Robert Greville, Lord Brooke, owner of Warwick Castle and Parliamentarian.

Brooke's arch rival, the Coventry recorder Spencer Compton, Earl of Northampton.

for their lives through the back door into the Bull Yard. Northampton then reported to the King. Coventry could now only go one way – for Parliament.

The next day, from the safety of Stoneleigh Abbey, King Charles issued a warrant demanding Coventry's subjugation:

> Charles R
>
> Whereas divers persons ill affected to his Matie's person and government, and strangers to his Cittie of Coventry, are lately gotten into that Cittie with armes and munic'on, who, with others of that place ill affected to the peace of this his Kingdome, have combyned to keepe the said Cittie by force of armes against his Matie, their Leige Lord and Soverein; for reducing of whom to their true obedience his Matie hath given orders to some Commanders of his Forces to assault the said Cittie, and by force to enter the same. Notwithstanding his Matie being verie unwilling, for some disaffected persons, to punish his good subjects and ruine his said Cittie, is graciously pleased thereby to declare. That in the case the said Strangers shall forthwith after the publishing of His Proclamac'on, depart peaceably out of the said Cittie, and they and the inhabitants presently lay down their armes, that then his Matie will pardon as well all the said Strangers, as all other the Inhabitants of the said Cittie. But if they shall persist in their said Acc'on of Rebellion, then his Matie is resolved to procccd against them as Traytors and Rebells, and to use all extremity for reducing the said Cittie to due obedience. Given at or Court at Stonely Abby the twentieth day of August, in the eighteenth yeare of our Reigne, 1642.

Next Warwickshire's noted historian Sir William Dugdale brought it forth, and after a short consultation he was informed that 'his Majesty's royal person should be most respectfully welcomed, but we could not with safety permit his cavaliers to enter the town.' It was shortly after revised: the King could enter, but with only 200 of his cavaliers. Charles, not a man to be dictated to, immediately decided to take the city by force and sent to Northampton for siege weapons. The army marched forth on Coventry and set up its cannon on Park Hill on the brow of Little Park Quarry. The King's tent is said to have been erected on the Mount, an artificial mount created in the Great Park in 1627.

King Charles I believed in the Divine Right of Kings and courted the Catholic faith.

Historical researcher Nicola Norman discovered a broadside entitled *Exceedingly Joyful News from Coventry* during her research. It was printed on 19 October 1642, from which we learn that under the date of 20 August 1642:

Upon Monday last there was information given to the house of Commons, by letters from Warwickshire, that his Majesty came to Coventry Saturday last, with a great number of cavaliers; his whole army consisted of about 6,000 horse, which the citizens of Coventry perceiving, they shut up the gates of the city, and stood upon their guard; whereupon his Majesty retired [back] to a knight's house about 3 miles from Coventry, and the cavaliers made the poor countryman's houses their inns, and then and there they made their own welcomes, taking what they pleased. His Majesty hath also caused warrants to be sent to the sheriff and others, officers of the county, to aid and assist him at his coming thither, but very few obliged him therein. He hath likewise caused the county to be summoned to appear before him on Monday next, when it is thought he intends to set up his standard, and that he is resolved to march with his forces for Warwick Castle, before which the Earl of Northampton lies with some forces, but hath little hope of gaining the same.

In *Certain Special and Remarkable Passages* the following statement occurs:

The Houses [of Parliament] also received letters informing them of the true state of things in Coventry. That his Majesty continued his siege and battered against the town from

A nineteenth-century engraving of how Coventry looked at the time of the Civil War.

Saturday till Monday last. That the cavaliers, with their pieces of ordnance, having battered down one of the gates, the townsmen, to prevent their entrance, stopped up the passage with harrows, carts, and pieces of timber, and with great courage forced the cavaliers (notwithstanding their ordnance) upon every attempt towards the gate soon to retreat, and that with some loss.

This may be an accurate report, for in John Vicars' *Parliamentary Chronicle,* written shortly after the event, it states:

The King ... drew up his forces before the city, planted his ordnance against its gate, which by continually playing thereon, at last they battered and brake open ... Not withstanding the valiant townsmen stoutly maintained the breech in the very mouth of the enemy's cannon ... and forced the cavaliers ... to retreat with loss every time ... and little or none to themselves, so thick and quick discharges they made upon them with their musquet shots ... before the gate was broken open, some shot of their cannon, not rightly levelled, beat down part of the Lady Hales house, in White-Fryers in the City. The said lady and an old woman, who had lain bed-ridden five years before in a place called the Tower, were both of them slain ... When the King's forces retired, the incessant shot of the city falling like hail upon them, these resolute citizens and soldiers, with one unanimous consent, sallied out of the city, and behaved in such a valiant undaunted manner, that they compelled the King's forces to retire with more than ordinary pace, forsaking their ordnance, which they cleared of all incumbrances, took two of them from the enemy, fiercely encountering the cavaliers and gave them such a shock and violent charge, that in a short time three score and

Above *Hollar's engraving of Sir William Dugdale, who carried Charles' warrant and fought for him in the streets of Kenilworth. (With kind permission of the Thomas Fisher Rare Book Library, University of Toronto.)*

Below *Kenilworth Castle in 1620.*

ten of them lay slain on the ground; the rest were forced to a shameful and hasty retreat from this unexpected attack on the citizens of Coventry.

The seventeenth-century historian John Rous claims one city defender died. He adds: 'If bookes, but true, and if Coventry men at Sturbridge fayre say true, that the King was not there, but the army was, and did not enter the town but shot into it, yet kild only one man ... the town issued out and slue diverse.'

During the engagement, which lasted three days, it is probably true that the King wasn't always there: in fact, he may have spent the entire engagement at Stoneleigh awaiting the city's subjugation so he could regally enter.

Meanwhile, from the south, Lord Brooke and Colonel Hampden were

leading a Parliamentarian army into Warwickshire consisting of 4,800 foot and eleven troops of horse. The advance was speeded up when Brooke received a message stating that the King was at Coventry and was 'playing' his ordnance on the city. As they approached the King was made aware that they were 10 miles away and decided a strategic withdrawal was in order. The King split his forces, heading for Nottingham and sending his main force south to hold back the Parliamentarian army. These were met at Southam and fifty men and horses were killed in a corn field. The King also left two companies at Kenilworth Castle. That evening he arrived at Nottingham, raised the royal standard, and the Civil War officially began.

Nehemiah Wharton, a subaltern officer with Lord Brooke's force, wrote on 30 August:

> Thursday, August 26th: our soldiers pillaged a malignant fellow's house in this City, and the Lord Brooke immediately proclaimed that whosoever should for the future offend in that kind shall have martial law. Fryday several of our soldiers, both horse and foote, sallied out of the City unto Lord Dunsmore's Parke and brought from thence great store of venison ... and ever since they make it their dayly practice ... This day our horsemen sallied out ... and brought in with them two cavaleers and with them an old base Priest, the parson of Sowe [Revd John Adrian of Walsgrave, a ancestor of John 'Fatty' Adrian, the prize fighter who appears later], near us and led him ridiculously about the city.

News came that Nuneaton had been had been put to the torch and 1,000 troops and a troop of horse marched with speed to the town, only to find that the enemy had fled. Wharton's regiment finally left the city at two in the morning in September after an alarm was raised.

Nearby Kenilworth Castle still held Royalists and Charles, fearing that the Parliamentarian strength was increasing, sent forth two troops of horse and one of dragoons to rescue them.

Sir William Dugdale led them through the back lanes. He later wrote:

> ...they came about ten o'clock at night to Kenilworth and ... marched out of that castle by seven of the clock the next morning. Nevertheless by intelligence given to the rebels in Coventry, such numbers of those with Horse and Foot pursued them, as that they were constrayn'd to make a stop in Curdworth Field to encounter them, when they charged these rebels (though five to one in number) so stoutly that they put them to the rout and took some of them prisoner.

Coventry was now under military rule and Warwickshire was controlled from Coventry; a permanent garrison was established in the city and Northampton, now a rebel, was officially replaced with Robert Devereux, Earl of Essex, as recorder in a ceremony in St Mary's Hall. A governor was appointed to control the garrison. Another siege was feared and Essex ordered more men and cannon to the city, which now held over 4,000 troops – to which a citizens' militia was added. Known Royalists were arrested, and those that fled had their property confiscated.

Prince Rupert, the King's nephew, began to harry the county and had already led an attack on Caldecote House. During this period this rather flash Prince – who was always accompanied by his large poodle, Boy – sent a letter to Coventry's new recorder kindly inviting him to a meeting:

My Lord, 23 Sept 1642,
I shall be ready, on his [King Charles'] behalf, to give you an encounter in a pitched field, the Dunsmore Heath, 10th October next. Or, I shall expect private satisfaction as willingly, at your hands for the same, and that performed by single duel. I know my cause to be so just that I need not fear; for what I do is agreeable both to the laws of God and

man. In the interim I am your friend till I meet you next.
Rupert

Essex chose not to take the impetuous Prince up on his challenge so Rupert instead brought the fight to Coventry. On 14 October 1642 another letter arrived asking the council to hand over the city to Rupert in the King's name. The city replied that, due to the 'inhuman acts of the cavaliers ... [and] how they ransacked and pillaged', the city was forced to deny his Majesty's desire.

Rupert and his cavalry chose to make an attack on the city. They were quickly repelled when they found twenty-six cannon firing on them – though some sources state that the Prince and his cavaliers actually entered the city and were blocked in narrow lanes by carts, forcing them to make a quick escape. Thereafter they fled back into the countryside and re-joined the King's force to take part in the inconclusive Battle of Edge Hill.

In 1643 Coventry was under the new governor, Colonel Alderman Barker, who wore jerkin and breastplate for his own security. It was decided that year, for the city's security, that many of the houses that stood outside the city gates would be dismantled. The timber frames and shingles of these buildings were stored in Trinity churchyard, to be later reused close by. Deep trenches were dug around the city and made floodable by sluices, and all the gates were stopped up except New Gate, Spon Gate, Bishop Gate, Greyfriars Gate and Gosford Gate. Outside these gates, trenches and half-circular

Prince Rupert of the Rhine, the King's nephew, who was the archetypical cavalier. Boy the poodle is pictured. (With kind permission of the Thomas Fisher Rare Book Library, University of Toronto.)

37

Gosford Gate during this period had a cannon added to its tower – no pitched roof then, and floodable defences outside. It also had a drawbridge. (Coventry Local Studies.)

ditches were dug and fortified with strong bulwarks and drawbridges. Primed cannon were placed on each gate and Barr's Hill was fortified.

In March that year, Lord Brooke passed through the city and his chaplain read from the text in the book of Esther: 'If I perish, I perish.' Brooke left Coventry for Lichfield, intending to destroy the cathedral. He planted cannon against the gate of the Cathedral Close and began to bombard the church. What he didn't know was that two men were hidden in the tower with fowling pieces. As Brooke stood in an open doorway, one fired upon him, sending a musket shot through his eye and into his brain, killing him instantly. On 19 March Spencer Compton, the outlawed city recorder, was killed at Hopton Heath. After being unhorsed and surrounded, he managed to kill

a colonel and several others before having his helmet struck off with the butt of a musket. He was summoned to surrender and replied, 'I scorn to take quarter from such base rebels as you.' No sooner did these words leave his mouth than he was struck from behind and killed with a single blow from a halberd.

On 3 April Rupert, with over 2,000 horse and foot, attacked Birmingham, putting many to the sword and burning eighty houses. After the attack it was reported that Rupert had called out, 'Where's your Coventry now? Where's your God Brooke now? You can see how your God fights against you!' A letter written at the time states, 'If Coventry had sent us what helpe it might, I believe the Enemy dost not have assaulted us.' The fact was that up until three days before the attack Coventry troops were in Birmingham. Rupert probably got word of their leaving, hence his taunts.

'The town was full of people that fled here for safety,' said a source from 1643, 'and the women of the city went forth to fill up the quarries, in the Great Park, so they couldn't harbour the enemy.' Being called together by the drum, the ladies, carrying mattocks and spades, marched forth to the park led by one Goodwife Adderley with a Hercules's club (a very large club) on her shoulder. The work ended when Mary Herbert fired a pistol. Two companies of foot manned the city wall every night and a constant guard was set by the Coventry Cross.

Basil Fielding, Earl of Denbigh later made city recorder in 1647

Basil Fielding, major-general of Coventry.
(With kind permission of the Thomas Fisher
Rare Book Library, University of Toronto.)

Forasmuch as this Citie is now filled with people, especially of strangers, amongst which some are separatists, and refuse to come to Church, and divers of them single women that work at their own hands. It is ordered that each Alderman of this Citie ... shall speedily inform themselves what and how many strangers in his Ward are now come to this Citie, and in whose houses and how employ'd; and also what separatist that come not to Church, and likewise of the single women as aforesaid to the end that such of them as shall be thought fit may be expelled the Citie.

became, in 1643, major-general of Coventry and commander in chief of Warwickshire, Worcestershire, Staffordshire and Shropshire. During 1643-4, he wintered his troops in the city; this caused many problems as the troops lacked discipline and continually brawled with the local garrison and populace.

The *City Annals* of 1644 state that the King seemed to be prevailing – and so once again the threat of siege returned. The population was again counted and found to be over 9,500. New towers were added to the walls, and large cannon mounted on them. With more and more coming into the safety of the walls, the city was starting to get crowded and it was thought necessary to reduce the population. Single women were therefore ejected from the city. On 24 July, the committee ordered that:

In 1645 the King took Leicester, which caused Coventry yet again to fear siege. A massive outwork was dug outside Gosford Gate, encompassing the river.

In that same year, in May, Oliver Cromwell himself was in the city. This was the first of three visits, which appear to have later been removed from the *City Annals* by Royalist scribes. On 14 July Cromwell smashed the King's army at Naseby, and Charles fled westwards. In 1646 eleven regiments of Scottish troops encamped by Gosford Green and remained there nearly a year. In this same year, as the Royalist army was no longer considered a threat, Parliament expressed a desire to dismiss Coventry's garrison. The garrison was sent to Ireland, leaving only 200 troops in the city. Peace, however, had not arrived.

The Second Civil War erupted in April 1648 with Royalist-instigated risings in Kent and Wales. In August a Scottish Royalist army marched south and were caught in a pincer movement by Cromwell at Preston. Half fled back to Scotland and the other half surrendered. Hundreds were brought back as prisoners to Coventry and imprisoned in such places as St John's church and the Leather Hall. Many people now believe the treatment of these prisoners is the root of the phrase 'sent to Coventry', although in truth this explanation was made up in the 1930s. It actually originates from a later incident, described in a later chapter.

In January 1649 the Scottish army sold King Charles to Parliament, and he was put on trial at Westminster Hall. His refusal to recognise those who judged him sealed his fate. He was found guilty and executed for tyranny. All seemed quiet. Then, in 1651, Prince Charles led a Scottish army into England. Coventry was put on alert, refortified and a regiment of foot put in place to protect it. On 25 August Oliver Cromwell arrived in the city, followed by his generals, Lambert and Harrison. When the Scottish army heard of the massive Parliamentarian force of 28,000 sitting outside Coventry it swung its course to the west and headed into Worcestershire. Cromwell followed and the armies clashed at Worcester.

An engraving of a famous painting of Oliver Cromwell, who came to Coventry on a number of occasions – lastly with a massive army to end the war.

Cromwell's New Model Army smashed the Royalist army, and Prince Charles fled, ending the war for good. A direct result of this conflict was that Coventry's magnificent city wall was demolished, by command of King Charles II, in 1662 – a punishment for daring to stand against his father.

AD 1665

STORMS, BLACK DEATH AND THE GREAT PLAGUE

COVENTRY, LIKE THE rest of this country, has historically experienced many weather extremes. While being blasted by wind, rain, lightning and drought, the citizens of the county weathered an even more dreadful menace – plague.

The *City Annals* record many major historical events in the city. Perhaps the earliest recorded unusual occurrence was in 1349, when we are informed that: 'This year was a great rain from Christmas to Midsummer, noe day, but it rained.' This inclement weather was followed by something even worse: the Black Death, as it came to be known – named after the black seeping lesions on its victim's skin. It came to Warwickshire in 1349 and did huge damage. William de Irreys, the Prior of St Mary's, fell victim. Afterwards an inquisition was held on the possessions of the priory and it was found that its tenants in the north of Coventry had been decimated by the pestilence; mills lay empty and derelict as no one survived to tend them. In 1350, the plague gets its second mention, '[a] great pestilence happened in this citty ... the living scarcely sufficed to

bury the dead.' A second version of the *Annals* states: 'When Churchyards were not sufficient and large enough to bury the Dead, then certain fields were purchased for that purpose.'

The year 1352, we are told, suffered yet more, as a dry summer, with no rain from March till the end of July, caused devastation to the crops. William Botoner was mayor of Coventry when it was reported, in 1359, that, 'a great pestilence and great winds happened that blew down steeples'. In 1364 and 1365 the Pope authorised William Greenburgh, Prior of Coventry, to ordain twenty-two-year-old monks as priests as so many of their elders had fallen victim to the Black Death.

Then, as a contrast to the drought of the Black Death era, the ice came in 1408, and a great frost covered the city and its surrounds, freezing everything for fifteen weeks and killing almost all of the small birds.

Other extremes appeared during the mayoralty of Richard Joy: 'September 28th 1426, between 1 and 2 in the morning, began a terrific earthquake which was universal; men thought that the Day of Judgement was come.

The Doom Painting in Holy Trinity church was created when it was feared the world was coming to its end. It depicts Christ judging the dead. Some go into heaven; others – including monks – are cast down into Hell's Mouth. (Holy Trinity church.)

The beasts of the field roared and drew to the towns with hideous noises, and the wild fowls of the air cried out.' A possible direct result of this event was the creation of one of Britain's most important Doom Paintings above the chancel arch of Holy Trinity church. In 1478 some copies of the *Annals* state that plague was again in force, slaughtering 4,450 Coventrians – almost a third of the total population.

In 1519, we are told of a sudden flood in Whitsun Week. The summer was so damp that it was called the 'wet summer'. The year 1540 was the opposite – no rain fell, making corn scarce. Plague returned in 1564, with 221 dead in the parish of St Michael. It returned again in 1575, when we are informed 'there dyed in Bablake

thirty persons. An old man helped to carry his daughter to her grave in St Michael's Churchyard, and no sooner had the funeral taken place than he fell down dead, and in three hours was buried in the same place.'

Just three years later plague returned again, though fewer people died in this outbreak. It was ordered by the Common Council that four men should be appointed weekly to bury the dead. They received 4 shillings a week and, to reduce the risk of infection, they were isolated in a barn off Hill Street. The plague continued into 1580 and the *Annals* recall: 'Ye 6th August a Great Earthquake, very terrible throughout England, & also Disease which swept many away. It was called the Speedy Repentance.' The earthquake may have actually caused damage to the spires of Trinity and St Michael as the *Annals* of that year makes a point of stating that they were re-pointed. The following year a comet was seen: 'A Commett & Great Smoake seen in the Air out of which came great flashes

A nineteenth-century engraving of St Michael's church, where some plague victims were buried. As it got worse larger isolated plague pits were dug. The tower and spire were shaken by an earthquake in 1580.

of fire.' Such sights, with the previous year's earthquake, made many of the good people of Coventry believe again the end of the world was nigh.

The last visitation of the plague in the sixteenth century took place in 1594. Nearly 18,000 people died in England. The plague ravaged Lichfield and Leicester, though Coventry seems to have escaped quite lightly: the *Annals* note 'butt one House visited in Coventry'. That year, however, ended with a great wind which caused much damage.

The year 1603-4 was less fortunate for the citizens of Coventry: 'A great plague [broke out] in this city, there died in all 585, of which 494 of the plague; almost all the inhabitants of Dead Lane died, which for that reason was so named, it being [previously] called St John's Street.' Anyone showing signs of infection was ordered to carry coloured rods when in public so they could be identified and avoided.

The *Annals* state that, in 1607, 'there happened an inundation which overflowed 250 dwelling-houses'. This flood is also recorded in *Stowe's Chronicles*. On Friday, 17 April 1607, as vouched for under the seal of Henry Sewell, mayor, the flood started in the early hours and was seen approaching the city from some miles away. The citizens were alerted and warned to save their goods, and within an hour the low-lying meadows and Coventry itself were under 9ft of water, which engulfed some 257 homes. The chronicle continues: 'it seemed so strange, considering that neither sea, nor any great river cometh near the ʼity, but only a small brook [the River

Sherbourne] half a yard deep at most, over which at all times of the year a man may either stride or leap.'

Lastly, the chronicle points out another anomaly about this flood: 'The rain and thunder decreased in about four hours. No one was drowned, but it left an abundance of snails.' Interestingly, later research has shown, around some of the coastline of England, traces of a mini-tsunami occurring at about this time!

The year 1615 had 'a very great Snow which lay 7 weeks, & the summer following proving very dry.' An even more unusual incident happened on the 9 July 1622:

> There happened such a thunder clap as is seldom heard. A little before it lightened exceedingly, and immediately a thunder bolt was seen to descend upon the Church [St Michael's] by those without. One Mr Marson, a stranger, was preaching, his text being, 'Be sober, and watch, for the end of all things is at hand,' which did strike much amazement and astonishment in the Congregation, that they verily thought the world had been at an end ... for upon the fall of the thunder bolt, there was a crack in one of the large pillars of the church.

The result of this was that a number of huge stones fell down from the tower and came smashing into the battlements of the church causing an almighty crash. Clumps of burning matter then fell amongst the church's congregation, much to their 'great astonishment'.

In 1625 the poor citizens of Coventry again suffered a visitation of the plague:

'Plague raged in Coventry; to avoid infection the inhabitants removed to houses built in the Grey Friars orchard, and near Quinton Pool, in the park.'

It seems that the actions of the mayor, William Burbage, and the city alderman that year – i.e. the removal of people out of infected areas – saved many and cut short the visitation. There is an interesting lease in the City Archive dated 20 September 1629 and relating to Alderman Henry Smyth and his brother Matthew and wife, Anne. They leased a cottage in Canley to Thomas Towers of Coventry, on lands occupied by Henry Smyth, with a very unusual clause, being: '[the right] to flee thither when there is plague in Coventry.'

Burials at Holy Trinity tell a sad tale of one family who fell victim: 'Oct. 7. 1625. A Childe of Ridlies in Welstreet; Oct. 10. 1625. A Childe of Ridlies in Welstreet; Oct. 21. 1625. An other childe of Ridlies; Oct. 26. 1625. An other childe of Ridlies; Oct. 27. 1625. Ridlie himself buried.' That's five members of one family buried in twenty days.

In 1636 the plague raged in London and Coventry put up its defences. Two watchmen were stationed at Newgate; one at Gosford Gate; one at Grey Friar's Gate; two at Spon Gate, and one at Bishop's Gate. The gates were kept open but the watchmen checked all who passed through them. Priory, Well, Cook, Hill, Cheylesmore, Little Park and Bastile gates were all closed day and night. Their wickets (a small door within the gates) were kept open, but they were attended by a warden.

Back to the extremes of weather: a few hot and cold spells were noted but nothing too 'off the scale' – though Charles I tried to blast his way into the city in 1642. The year 1647 was a wet year, causing the price of corn to spiral; 1652 had a very dry summer. On 14 January 1665, meanwhile, 'a terrible wind blew down Trinity steeple by the fall of which the Church was broke down and one boy killed.' The burial of the boy himself took place in Trinity churchyard: 'January 24th 1665. Jacob Astaley, born at Stichell [Stivichall], killed by the fall of the Church spire.' The following year we are informed that, by the diligence of Mr Thomas King (landowner and brewer) and Mr Thomas Bewdley (landowner and plumber) and other members of the parish, work began on the restoration of the tower, spire and parts of the damaged church. The spire itself – said to be bigger and 'better made' – was finally finished in 1668. The work may not have been so good, however, for it had to be taken down and rebuilt in 1675.

Holy Trinity spire was, in 2012 at least, the home to a breeding pair of peregrine falcons, who have been in the city for about ten years. However, they are currently vacationing from St Michael's tower, which is covered by scaffolding – much to the consternation of these fabulous birds.

In February 1795 heavy rain, combined with the quick thawing of thick snow, caused areas up to West Orchard to disappear under 4ft of water. There was worse to come in February 1830, a particularly cold period. The *Coventry Mercury* reported: 'On Wednesday last, an inquest was held at the Buck & Crown, Radford, near this City, on the body of Thomas Newbold of Coundon, who was found dead in a field on Tuesday morning. When found the body was covered with snow. It was supposed he fell down from weakness and infirmity on Monday night and was frozen to death. The deceased was 71 years of age. Verdict, found dead.'

The year 1665 also saw another massive outbreak of the plague in London, and again precautions were taken. It was ordered that a guard was to be kept at the gates from 6 a.m. to 9 p.m. to prevent 'wandering persons' from entering the city. By July plague had increased in the capital and it was ordered that no person from London should be allowed to enter the city. No coach or horseman was allowed to pass through without being accompanied by a warden. It was also ordered that any Londoner who had been in the city for less than a month should leave under pain of imprisonment. Citizens were appointed to watch the gates constantly and any inhabitant of the city who had received a visitor or goods from London would have to pay a warder, who would be placed at their door to keep them in. All these precautions were not surprising – in London an estimated 68,596 people died of the plague in that year alone.

This era finished with Coventry close to starvation, as the year 1673 saw another weather extreme: 'Last year was so wet that it rained more or less every day for many months altogether.

So great [a] snow in Februarie [1674] which was also driven with the wind that travailers could not pass, so were frozen to death, and others lost in the snow. Winter continued so long that oats and barley could not be sowed ... Corn very dear here.'

In 1679 a hail storm in London was thought fit to be mentioned in the *Annals*, as the stones were described as measuring between 10in and 12in around!

Coventry again suffered in 1683 with 'an earthquake', followed by 'ye great frost': 'It began to freeze in September. The Great Frost began Nov. 20. 1683 and continued till Ladyday 1684.' Many animals died, and spades and ploughs could not penetrate the ground. In this year a fair was held on the frozen River Thames – it is now thought, by some, that Britain was actually in a miniature Ice Age. In 1686, '3,000 inhabitants died, the food being spoiled by the hot summer and a long frost'. This is probably a massive exaggeration, but many seemed to have died. The last calamity recorded in the *City Annals* was the cracking of St Michael's spire by a lightning strike in 1694.

AD 1754

MURDER MOST FOUL

SOME YEARS AGO I was given a handwritten document by a lady who was leaving Coventry to go and live in Spain. The four-sided folio sheet was written by Alderman John Hewitt, three times mayor of Coventry and the city's most notable magistrate and thief-taker. Hewitt published his journal in 1779. It was based on his years in Coventry in pursuit of criminals. A personal friend of the great London thief-taker Sir Henry Fielding, Hewitt sent a number of criminals to the gallows.

An extract from the original document written in Alderman John Hewitt's hand. Hewitt was a one-man police force and Coventry's greatest thief-taker.

The document is written in exactly the same style as Hewitt's journal but this particular piece was never finished and never made it into his book. It begins, 'From the *Coventry Mercury*, 22 July 1754':

On Saturday morning about eleven o'clock the body of a young man, genteely dressed, above five foot six inches in length, with a round face, a large pock hole on the left side of his upper lip, a small one over it, and a few on his forehead, was found by some hay makers, covered with hay, about forty yards from the footpath in the third close on the other side of Whitley Mill, about a mile from this city, barbarously murdered and robbed. He had on a dark brown wig, a light coloured fustian frock [coat] with plated buttons and brown linen waistcoat and breeches called nankeen with buttons of the same colour; blue grey stockings, his shoes and hat taken off. An old pair of shoes with plain iron or steel buckles in them, the soles of which were sewed ... with wire. An ordinary old hat torn at the edges with some holes ... a small hazel stick with a round turned box head ... and a hedge stake lay at the side of him, with which stake it is thought he was murdered. His head was very much bruised and broke but no other wounds as yet appear. His breeches pockets were found inside out.

H. Miles of Little Brickhill wrote a letter, dated 4 August 1754, to Joseph Hewitt, Coventry's town clerk. It reads:

The young man that was found murdered near Coventry, as appears by the description given, lay at William Page's at the Cross Keys on Wednesday evening the 17 July in company with a man that appeared like a chairman [i.e. a man who carried sedan chairs, an early form of taxi] having a large blue great coat ... He was an ill looking man and was much in liquor, but the young man was very sober and said he picked up his companion on the road, who pretended he was going to see his father, who he said lived near Coventry, which said place they intended to reach the next day. They accordingly set out next morning between 5 & 6 o'clock and were directed to call at the Duke of Marlborough's Head at Stoney Stratford ... but the young man told his companion ... that he would leave him for that it did not suit his pocket or constitution to drink as he did.

Hewitt himself continues:

The young man who was on Saturday 20 July found murdered proves to be one William Presbury and lived with one Mr Howes, a carrier upon London Wall, was going to see his friends who lived at Hawardine, Flintshire.

His father is said to be a blacksmith there. He is supposed to be robbed of a silver watch with a tortoise shell case, stubbed with silver, a pair of wrought oval silver shoe buckles, a silver stock buckle, a shirt stock, white cotton pair of stockings, a blue and white hanker-chief, a red and yellow silk one, and a pair of single channel pumps, money and diverse other things ... Note there is a reward of forty pounds payable by Act of Parliament on the conviction of every Highway Robber.

The investigation moves on to 9 June. Hewitt notes that the young man was robbed and murdered in July and at last a discovery of the persons concerned 'in this horrid villainy is likely to be brought to light.'

He goes on to say that a miller who lived between Tamworth and Lichfield had read the previous notice in the paper and had informed Hewitt that he had purchased the watch from one Woodcock of Tamworth for two guineas. It appeared that Woodcock was a villain and had been transported at the last assizes at Stafford, three weeks since, in the company of two brothers by the name of Parliamane. The pocket watch was secured and one of the Parliamane brothers was found to be in Warwick Gaol; the other was in London's Bridewell. It was noted that the things Woodcock was in possession of actually belonged to the young man who had been murdered. Woodcock was sent for, 'to be made an example of.'

Hewitt continues from Coventry on 16 June:

The Bridge and Old Mill, Whitley

Whitley Mill, on Whitley Common, a short distance from where Presbury's body was found.

On Saturday last was examined at Birmingham by Justice Wyrely, John Parliamane who bought a watch off Woodcock that he afterwards sold to the miller and which proves to be William Presbury's who was murdered on the 18 July last. At the same time was examined Thomas Griffiths, a labourer who says that the shoes which were found by the murdered man were formerly his and that Woodcock lay with him [it was not uncommon in the eighteenth century for strangers to share a tavern rooms when travelling] about a week before the said murder ... and got up betimes in the morning and picked his pocket of 4 or 5 shillings, stole his landlord's hat, took his shoes instead of his own.

Parliamane stated that Woodcock had the hat, shoes, stockings, handkerchief and watch of the murdered man; he also had two 36 shilling pieces, several guineas and 30 shillings in silver.

B. Heene wrote to Hewitt from Fenny Stratford on 18 June 1755:

John Woodworth's account of Woodcock ... description agrees with that in your letter that he robbed him of his hat ... likewise the person he lay with of a pair of shoes and some money and confessed himself that he had been a profligate fellow and overrun his friends ... Also George Wykes at the Red Lion & Dolphin at Fenny Stratford says he employed Woodcock in mowing and making hay for he did not care to trust him in his house, he having villainous a look and so bad a character he stole the victuals and wallet from a labourer. Woodworth and Wickes describe him; about 5 foot 7 inches high, a dark coloured coat, red waistcoat and breeches, thin visage, sharp nose, freckled face, straight long hair and stoops in the shoulders.

That is the end of the document – as Hewitt didn't record the result of these events in his published journal we have no record of its outcome. There is only one record of a (James) Woodcock being executed this year in Chelmsford; if this is our man I know not. Presbury was likely to have been buried in the nearest local church – unless, of course, his family claimed his remains.

The end came suddenly to a young and genteel William Presbury over 250 years ago, at the hands of a villain on Whitley Common; he may be long gone, but now he is not forgotten.

A SOLDIER'S LIFE

BEFORE COVENTRY HAD its own barracks it was a garrison city, regularly taking in hundreds of troops every year. Officers were garrisoned in the best inns while the common foot soldiers tended to be garrisoned in the commoner inns and with the civilian population.

During the close of 1756 General Stewart's regiment, the 37th Foot, were based in the city. It was reported on 6 December that, as five companies were to leave for neighbouring market towns, a gunsmith was called in to examine the condition of their muskets. He declared 'that they were so crooked in the barrels that, if you was to shoot a ball out of them upon a line, before it flew 200 yards it would enter the earth; and that he believes the firelocks of the whole regiment are the same.'

The presence of troopers in the city was sometimes quickly felt. On 23 March 1757, for example, the *Coventry Mercury* reported, 'In a public house in this city on Saturday night last a fray happened between a soldier and two other men, in which the soldier cut one of the men with a hanger [a broad-bladed, slightly curved sword] in the face, in so desperate a manner that his life is despaired of. The Watchmen coming in the soldier struck at 'em and accidently cut off one of his fingers...'

A similar incident happened in January 1772 at the Unicorn near the Coventry Cross, the base of which – despite what most local history books tell us – was still standing. Here a certain Adam Tilley of Barby had spent the evening drinking in the company of billeted Corporal Jackson of the 4th Dragoons and a few of his men. Tilley, as he was passing through the city, spent several shillings on supplying the soldiers with drink after they had agreed he could share their room for the night. When

A soldier or Redcoat from the mid-eighteenth century, when General Stewart's regiment were billeted in the city.

The entrance to Coventry Barracks, built in 1792, from Smithford Street.

– and vices. Robbery, gambling, drinking and womanising were the orders of the day. Like all garrison towns, Coventry suffered from a sudden sharp rise in pregnancies, the result of a local girl and a fancy uniform. I know, for it happened to my great-grandmother, who was tempted by a smile and a flash of a Royal Artillery jerkin from Coventry Barracks. Luckily she settled down and married another Royal Artillery soldier from the barracks – my great-granddad, who, despite surviving the Afghan and Egyptian wars, was nearly shot in Broadgate in 1893 by an out-of-control watchmaker!

Back to those early soldiers: their general misbehaviour led to the creation of the saying 'sent to Coventry' – they were shunned by the

it was time to retire, Corporal Jackson twice refused Tilley entry to the room and when Tilley complained that he had been ill-used, Jackson, with no provocation, drew his sword and ran Tilley through seven times. Tilley died soon afterwards. Jackson was secured. The outcome is unknown to me, and will probably remain a mystery: in these times matters such as this were dealt with by the military and not in public courts. As the newspaper fails to report any consequences, however, the officer probably – literally – got away with murder.

Coventry in the eighteenth century was a city where hundreds of armed soldiers loitered – troops were only occupied through part of the day in reviews and training. The rest of the time they were left to their own devices

The Unicorn Inn stood close to Coventry Cross at the junction of Broadgate and Cross Cheaping.

ANOTHER INFAMOUS DEATH IN 1772

Perhaps one of Coventry's strangest and most infamous deaths occurred in the same year that Corporal Jackson murdered Mr Tilley: a case of spontaneous human consumption.

The case was reported in the *Coventry Mercury* in March 1772. 'On Monday last,' it reported, 'the Coroner's Inquest sat on the remains of Mrs Clews, a widow, in Gosford Street in this city, who was found early on the said morning, burnt to death, and brought in their verdict, accidental death.'

> Various are the opinions concerning this unhappy woman's fate, for when she was found, there was nothing remaining but her head, thighs, and legs, the rest of her body being consumed to ashes. But by all, it is agreed, she was a great drinker of liquors, and smoker of tobacco and it is conjectured by some people, that being intoxicated with liquor, she had lighted her pipe when in bed and that some sparks of fire from it set fire to the bed-cloths; and by others it is thought that being very much intoxicated with liquor, she in attempting to smoke, the fire catched her breath and consumed her inwardly, before it catched the bed, as the room was not much damaged, and part of the bed, &c. remained unburnt.

It is said that the smoke issuing from her room attracted a neighbour, who broke the door down. Mary – or what remained of her, namely her legs – lay on the floor. As is typical in such cases, the furniture in the room was only slightly damaged and the bedstead only superficially burned, and none of the blankets damaged. The phenomena we know as spontaneous combustion is still unexplained, but what is certain is that each case is capable of creating a heat so intense it can almost completely destroy a human body, yet leaves the surroundings almost untouched. To add to the mystery, the *Mercury* concludes:

> There was a very uncommon thing happened, especially at this season of the year, when the remains of this unfortunate woman was going to the place of internment in Stoke Church Yard on Wednesday last, being accompanied the whole of the way by great numbers of flies which surrounded the coffin whenever it was moved out of the house, and continued about it till put in the hearse, and were very troublesome to the horses, and continued flying about them and the hearse till what remained of her was put underground.

local population. Things did improve with the building of the barracks in 1792, but back in March 1756, while Colonel Lambton's regiment was billeted in the city, the council itself offered a guinea over-and-above the commanding officer's bounty to any Coventry citizen who joined the regiment. This was not done simply through the goodness of the council's heart – it was a ploy used to encourage the 'lower orders' to join up and leave the city, thus cutting the crime rate and the general disorder that blighted the area. On this occasion, having but little take-up, the council, under Alderman John Hewitt, even offered an extra two guineas to any Freeman who enlisted.

This encouragement, and the offering of bounty money, had its drawbacks, as many men, plied with alcohol (which was an important part of the enlistment process), took the bounty and signed up. These recruits, when sober, often regretted their actions, leading many to desert. Desertion in the British Army in this period, and in the nineteenth century, was endemic: my own great-great-grandfather, Coventry-born Thomas Bradnick, deserted twice from the Duke of York's Regiment in 1826. For this offence he could have received up to 200 lashes, but he, like many, returned to their regiment. His desertion didn't ultimately affect Thomas, for he rose in the ranks and became the colour sergeant of the 2nd Battalion, 60th Rifles, and from 1848 until his retirement he was a paid sergeant and paymaster of the 1st Warwickshire Militia.

Those who chose to desert seventy years before met a different response. At the beginning of 1757 we hear of eight deserters from Stewart's regiment: William McCartney, age thirty-two, a husbandman born in Ireland, with brown hair, rough-faced, 'shy look', ran off in a blue coat; Thomas Stenson, age twenty-four, well made and wearing a greatcoat; John Vaughan, husbandman, aged twenty-six, went off in a dark-coloured coat and blue breeches; John Edwards, aged nineteen, from Orton, Warwicksire; Thomas Moore, age twenty-one, born in Stratford; John Sharman, aged forty-six, from Seckwell, who had several moles on his face, was a little bald on the crown, and deserted in a light brown surtout coat; John Hillman, aged twenty-six,

Coventry Barracks in the 1880s. At this time it was occupied by Royal Artillery regiments. My own great-grandfather is one of these men.

LOOK OUT, 2ND BATTALION!

In July 1905 an inquest was held in the Old Mayoress's Parlour (Draper's Room) in St Mary's Hall on the death of Samuel Potter, who was killed at the Radford Butts. Potter, of No. 10 Primrose Hill Street, was a member of the 2nd Battalion, Royal Warwickshire Regiment, commanded by Col. William Wyley. Potter, who had been a volunteer for many years, had fought in Egypt and the Boer War and had previously been cautioned for looking over the parapet when marking. On this occasion it appears he did it for the last time, for he took a bullet through the jaw and then the brain, which killed him instantly.

a red-headed tailor who liked the uniform enough to run off in his full regimentals; and Thomas Meeks, aged twenty-four, a locksmith by trade who enlisted in Coventry and was described as full-faced, brown hair and well made with two 'remarkable cuts', one under each eye. Soon after, Alderman Hewitt offered 20 extra shillings, over and above the bounty, for their capture. Few deserters were captured at this time, despite such promises.

In March 1757, courts martial were held in Coventry on two men from Stewart's regiment. One of the men had deserted several times already. His fate was sealed, for on 18 April it was reported: 'On Saturday last, about noon, a soldier belonging to General Steuart's Regiment, quartered in this city, was shot for desertion in the Park. He had been condemned to be shot for desertion once before, and was reprieved. --- He behaved very penitent and acknowledged he deserved to die.'

The punishments continued, for on 27 June we are informed: 'On Wednesday morning last a soldier belonging to Gen. Steuart's Regiment received a thousand lashes, and was afterwards drummed out of the regiment with a halter about his neck for desertion.'

The *Coventry Mercury* also informed its readers, under the same date:

On Saturday last, George Robinson (of the said regiment) was shot in the Park for desertion being an old offender. He died very penitent and in a manner very much becoming a person in his unhappy circumstances. He desired the soldiers to take warning by his untimely end, and to avoid keeping company with lewd women, to whom he chiefly attributed his death, saying he had often sold his linen, &c, to supply them with money, and then being afraid to face his officers, was the occasion of his deserting. It is thought another soldier who is now in custody, and was to have been shot about eight months ago, but reprieved, and has since deserted [and] will be shot when the regiment gets into camp.

The place of execution for these men was against the city wall by Little

Park Gate at the end of Little Park Street. Where the men were buried, however, history does not record. The punishment of soldiers continued in the city unabated. The *Coventry Mercury* reported the following on 31 October 1830:

> On Tuesday morning a Courts Martial was held in the City, on two privates belonging to the 60th Rifles Regiment [my great-great-grandfather's regiment], which passed through here on their march to Carlisle. One of them was charged with selling his ammunition and the other with having stolen £5 from his comrade. They were both found guilty and received 300 lashes.

This punishment may have taken place in the barracks – although, as the regiment was passing through and the 5th Dragoons were stationed in the barracks, the Rifles may have camped in the Great Park.

The use of Coventry as a garrison city certainly left its mark: we still have a 'Barracks car park' built upon the site of the old barracks. Soldiers who died here still lie in our churchyards; the gravestone of Daniel John Hanley, a twenty-year-old member of the King's Light Dragoons, can be seen in St Michael's churchyard bearing the tools of his trade: a rifle, pistol and sword. The stone was placed there by his regiment to honour a good friend and soldier. Two others – Edward Drury and Moses Baker, dragoons of Lord Pembroke's regiment – graced Gibbet Hill for nigh on forty years, their bodies tarred and encased in the iron of a gibbet cage for the crime of murder. It's no wonder the city had such a love-hate relationship with soldiers!

AD 1780-1832

YELLOWS VS BLUES

The Strange and Surprising History of Coventry's Elections

OVENTRY'S ELECTIONS, IN the past, were synonymous with bribery and with sheer bloody violence. In fact, many of Coventry's most violent events took place at the poll booth. The niceties of politics didn't always apply as you literally fought your way to power in Coventry.

For example, the *Coventry Mercury* of 4 December 1780 has this to say:

> Whereas a great number of Ruffians and Clodhoppers, who were hired by a certain noble Lord with a design by force and violence to beat and drive away the Freemen who were peaceably assembled round the booth on Wednesday morning last; but were by the manly and glorious resistance of the said Freemen dispersed and driven to their affright into various parts of the country, and not have been since heard of. This is therefore to give notice that if the said ruffians and Clodhoppers will return to C-mb A-b-y, they shall receive a free pardon for their cowardice ... should anyone find any such unhappy creatures wandering about ... give information to

the said noble Lord, so that they may be conducted to their several habitations.

You probably guessed the noble Lord was Lord Craven of Combe Abbey.

It appears that these over-active elections started in the city at the time of the Restoration in 1660, when Major Robert Beake, ex-mayor and noted Parliamentarian officer, was one of four candidates to run for the two seats in Parliament representing the city. For some unknown reason the election was declared void and another was held a few months later. After 'considerable strife' it was won by William Jesson.

The election of 1705 between Edward Hopkins and Sir Orlando Bridgeman for the Whigs, and Sir Christopher Hales and military officer Thomas Gery for the Tories, saw an attempt to control the problem. The mayor, a Whig called Samuel Billing, was co-founder of a charity school. Three months before the election there had been riots in the city and threats made. Billing approached the Queen and the secretary of state and acquired a government injunction

THE KING'S BLUES, OR LOYAL FOXHUNTERS.

An eighteenth-century political cartoon showing Coventry and its spires beyond a political hunt – a lot closer to the truth than one would imagine.

banning the carrying of sticks and the gathering of large groups during elections. His opponents, Hopkins and Bridgeman, appeared to agree to this but Tory and deputy lieutenant Thomas Gery told the mayor that he had a share of power and intended on using it. 'If the Mayor brought the Constables [to keep the peace],' he said, 'he would raise his men, and they should bring sticks and he would take care of the peace.'

Despite the threat, the mayor brought in the constables and doubled the watch sitting up all night. At about 3 a.m. Gery began to raise his men, 500 of whom fell unexpectedly upon the magistrates, constables and watch at 5 a.m. The peacekeepers were assaulted, disarmed and driven off, and the mayor wounded. Gery's colleague Sir Christopher Hales then 'joyned them and marched about the City in a riotous

manner till 9 of the clock, and then they possessed themselves of the [St Mary's] Guildhall.' The Tories held the hall for three days armed with thick cowl staffs. A poll of a sort took place, but hundreds were refused entry – and many were literally dragged out of the hall. One Lightburn was attacked so viciously that he was thought to be dead by the time he was carried from the building, and another man, called Bates, so badly beaten that he spent a month in bed recovering after the vote. The Whig candidates attempted to get into the hall, but in vain. Utterly corrupt, the sheriffs allowed this state of affairs to continue. When inspectors were proposed for the count, Gery pointed to the mob, saying, 'There are our inspectors.' Not surprisingly, the Tories were declared the victors. However, their victory lasted but a short time, and a judge soon declared the count

*In 1705 election votes were taken in the
Guildhall – if you could get in. It was held by
armed Tory supporters for three days.*

void. Various notables were warned
that no such scenes would be tolerated
at the re-election, and the count that
followed – known as the 'peaceable
election' – went to the Whigs.

The election of 1713 was based
in the old Gaol Hall in Pepper Lane.
Outside its door, several supporters of
John Neale of Allesley Park, a Whig,
were assaulted and humiliated by
being placed on the back of a large,
sharp-backed wooden horse. Sir
Christopher Hales and Sir Frederick
Skipwith were declared the victors
and afterwards several hundred
Freeman complained of these and
other 'indirect practices ... and
likewise the great riots.' The election
stood nonetheless.

The use of violence to win elections
remained in full swing in the years
that followed. The Corporation and

the Whig party were represented in
the 1722 election by Sir Adolphus
Oughton and John Neale of Allesley.
Against them were the Tories Sir
Fulwar Skipwith and the Honorable
Fulwar Craven, brother of Earl Craven
of Coombe Abbey. An account written
at the time gives us an excellent
description of events:

The Tories endeavoured to return
their men using violence; sticks and
clubs were provided from Warwick,
and elsewhere, and whole horse loads
of them were brought into Coventry
before the election, or taken to
Coombe Abbey, where many persons
were armed on Saturday and Monday.
On the last day Lord Craven and his
friends marched into the City, at the
head of 2,000 men, horse and foot,
with green twigs and leaves in their
hats, armed, colours flying, drums
beating and trumpets sounding.
They began rioting, smashed many
windows, stayed those who had no
colours ... At the Cross a luckless
sheriff was directing the rebuilding of
the [polling] booth --- he was seized,
knocked down, wounded, and had
his head broken; but the constables
coming from the Mayor's Parlour
effected his rescue, and seized an
offender, but not before thirty of
their number were seriously hurt.
At the wish of the Mayor, one of the
Alderman went to the steps of the
[Coventry] Cross and read the Riot
Act, but was prevented, and had to fly
for his life; whereupon the mob pulled
up the paving stones, and smashed the
glass and woodwork of the windows
of their opponents' houses.

The election itself was much the same, with the Tories driving the Whigs away. They regrouped in the Women's Market Place, took the booth and polled first, before being set upon by the Tories – who by this point were armed with sticks and staves. As the mayor, John Kilsby, fled to his house, he was hit by a stone; an alderman was beaten after trying to stop a group of men taking the mayor's gate off its hinges! The winning faction seems rather irrelevant, but nonetheless this round went to the Whigs, supported by the Corporation.

The election of 1780 was described by one later writer as 'an exciting contest'. Polling at the booth in Cross Cheaping started quietly, but it wasn't to last. Within half an hour of opening a group of 500 'Blue Freemen' (Tories) marched on the booth, driving the 'Yellow Freemen' – Corporation-supported Whigs – away. The poll closed at one o'clock with twenty-three votes for the Tories, Yeo and Holroyd, and four for Whigs Halifax and Rogers. Voting was resumed on Monday, and the Corporation enlisted around 700 colliers, roughs and prize-fighters as constables, to – as they cynically claimed – 'preserve the peace'. Again, access to the booth was crucial, and at the end of the day it was thirty-four to Holroyd and Yeo and twenty-one to Halifax and Rogers.

On 16 September the sheriffs promised they would control voting and that the Freeman would be polled alternately, one by one. All was well – or was it? The following day, Sunday, saw the Corporation arming hundreds more in St Mary's Hall with staves. They were then instructed to take the booth on Monday and hold it for half an hour – just long enough to poll enough Yellow Freeman to tip the balance for Halifax and Rogers. Then, at this point, the sheriffs were to declare a riot and under that pretext close the booth. That night, however, it was the Blues who took possession of the booth.

Monday morning began with the Yellows leading a full attack on the booth while an alderman led a group of armed constables and partisans from the Mayor's Parlour. Staves and fists flew as hundreds clashed: the Yellows were driven back and the chief constable crushed underfoot. The Blues chased a large numbers of Yellows, mainly consisting of colliers, into St Mary's Hall – though eventually the main gate was closed against them. Meanwhile, the Blues gathered around the corner in White Horse Yard and threw lumps of smashed paving stones through the beautiful fifteenth-century stained glass windows, the work of master Coventry artist John Thornton.

The scheming failed: the sheriffs closed the booth after only ninety-six Freemen had been polled, leaving hundreds un-polled. Afterwards the Tories complained to the House of Commons about the sheriff's behaviour and 1,192 signed a declaration of their support of Holroyd and Yeo, insisting that through violence they were prevented from voting. The Whigs also blamed the violence for their lack of votes and the sheriffs certified that they were unable to proceed through riot. The election was therefore declared void.

A second election was held on 29 November, with the same candidates. The Corporation engaged a large number of constables, ruffians and prize-fighters from Bedworth, Birmingham and Atherstone, and many of Lord Craven's tenants and labourers were sworn in privately at Stoke. The Blue Freemen surrounded the booth on opening and soon the Corporation-supported Yellows entered, following the constables who came up six abreast from the Women's Market. Each constable carried a heavy pole 6ft long and a stave 2ft long tipped with an iron knob painted with the city's arms. Just in case, each man also carried a bludgeon.

They demanded the booth. The Yellows refused; pushing at the front began and a countryman had his stick pulled from his grip. A general 'bloody melee' ensued. Some of Lord Craven's tenants – who had been pressed into service probably against their wishes – threw down their staves. This caused panic amongst the Yellows, who were stoned as they fled out of the Market Square. During this flight their sheer numbers made it difficult to get through the small archway by the Mayor's Parlour. Finally, however, they got through and a chase ensued down Cross Cheaping and West Orchard. Many hid in the river under the arches of the houses that stood above. Only fifty-seven votes were balloted.

Thereafter the Blues guarded the booth on a number of nights and made official complaints about the Corporation's armed non-voters. Arrangements were made for all to vote, one by one. This was agreed – but the Corporation had other ideas. Instead, they decided to create what came to be known as 'Mushroom Freemen'. To vote in Coventry at this time you had to have served a seven-year apprenticeship within 3 miles of St Mary's Hall. Coventry had a population of around 10,000, of which less than 1,000 men were eligible to vote. The Corporation decided that, as they were in danger of losing, they would increase their own candidate's votes by swearing in more Freemen – whether or not they filled the criteria. At a meeting in St Mary's Hall, Mayor Pickin surreptitiously swore in sixty-six Freeman, none of whom qualified for Freemanship and many of whom were total strangers who actually had to ask for directions to the hall. In total, 266 new voters were sworn in over three days: these included silk weavers from Mile End, London, weavers from Oxford and soldiers from Portsmouth and Derbyshire – to name just a few.

The Blues protested against these totally illegal Yellow Freemen but the Corporation kept sending them to the polls. When the Blues tried to drive them back the Corporation sent in the heavy squad, beating and battering their way to the booth. The sheriffs who had worked against the Blue vote read the Riot Act and the poll ended. The sheriffs then declared the election for Sir Thomas Halifax and Thomas Rogers: the illegal Mushroom vote had won. Or had it? Shortly afterwards, Yeo and Sheffield petitioned against the sheriffs' return. Halifax and Rogers claimed that it was a fair election. The House of Commons considered the petition, supplemented with damning evidence, and pointed out that while Corporation voters were allowed normal entrance to the polling booth, the opposition were forced to climb a precariously placed ladder to simply get into the booth! The Commons concluded that the Mushrooms and their votes were illegal and the election was given to Yeo and Sheffield. The sheriffs' part in this absurdity was then looked into, with the result that they were sent to Newgate Prison, occupying the condemned cell as the prison had been damaged by fire in the recent Gordon Riots. Despite this incarceration, throughout the rest of the eighteenth century the violence continued – as did the sudden appearance of Mushrooms. Other incidents included the tarring and feathering of Richard Oldham in the 1785 election.

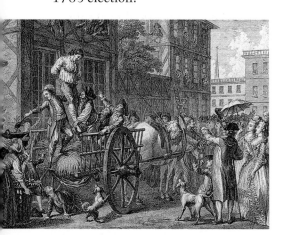

Tarring and feathering in action. (John Malcolm, depicted here, was attacked at Boston at the beginning of the Wars of Independence.) (LC-USZC4-4604)

One particularly nasty incident occurred during the 1802 election between Whigs Barlow and Jeffreys and Tories Bird and Moore. During this election, my great-great-great-uncle Sir Skears Rew, acting sheriff, apparently had a rough time of it at the election booth, as did his aide Issac Love. A letter written by Mayor John Mullis on 6 August 1802, states:

On the morning of the 22 July, the chairing of Mr Jeffreys and Captain Barlow [supported by the Corporation] ... took place [chairing was the carrying of candidates through the streets on a chair, whilst their supporters cheered them on]. The Band of the Regiment, at the request of several of the principal inhabitants, attended the procession. Several of the Privates, about sixteen in number (unarmed) assisted in leading the horses of the band, WHO CONDUCTED THEMSELVES THROUGHOUT THE DAY IN THE MOST ORDERLY AND PEACEABLE MANNER. On the procession entering Spon-street A VERY LARGE MOB of persons, in the interest of Mr Bird and Mr Moore (the unsuccessful Candidates) were assembled for the avowed purpose of attacking and insulting the Members. The chair of Mr Jeffreys was soon surrounded ... stones thrown ... and at length such acts of riot and violence committed ... An attempt was made by a mob to dismount one of the Band, which was resented by the Privates leading the horse, and some blows were struck on both sides. Had not the attack been made on the Band, not a soldier would have stirred from his post.

Later on that day a mock chairing was held in Radford, which was then a small village nearly attached to Coventry. A large crowd of about 1,000 supporters of Bird and Moore marched from Radford to Coventry. The mayor's letter continues:

> About half past seven or eight o'clock, the BANDITTI returned from Radford to Coventry, preceded by two drums and two fifes insulting and beating every person they met wearing a cockade of Mr Jeffreys or Captain Barlow. The malice of the mob was particularly aimed at the military. A soldier at the Market-place was violently beaten by them, thrown down, and cruelly beaten. On their approaching the Barracks, the Rouge's March was beat and several of the Privates standing there were attacked ... Many of the inhabitants were also seriously hurt ... A small detachment of the military [Captain Barlow's men] was therefore ordered out, and the mob instantly dispersed ... I HAVE NOT HEARD of any serious injury happening to anyone. It may be true that SOME BOYS RECIEVED BLOWS GIVEN OVER THE SHOULDERS by the flat side of the sword, but no information HAS REACHED MY EAR of any person being SERIOUSLY WOUNDED or EVEN WOUNDED AT ALL.
>
> J. Mullis, Mayor.

That was the mayor's version of the event. A second record, however, survives – and it is at variance with this. Mr Moore sent to Colonel Brownrigg an extract from a communication he had received from Mr T. Mason, a Coventry solicitor. He pointed out that Mr Mason was a gentleman of great worth and unsullied integrity. Mason wrote:

> Yesterday was the day appointed for chairing Messrs Barlow and Jeffreys, during the whole of which the soldiers belonging to Captain Barlow's regiment (the King's Own or 1st Dragoon Guards) were extremely riotous and most unmercifully beat ... many of the inhabitants without the smallest provocation. ... In the evening, without the smallest appearance of riot or disturbance the troops were let loose from the Barracks, first one by one (mounted and swords drawn) and afterwards in a body, headed by Cornets Addison and Bracebridge, during which the most wanton cruelty ever known was practiced on the peaceful inhabitants. The troops indiscriminately cut and hewed down men, woman and children, forced themselves into houses, and brutally beat the persons therein. In fact it is impossible for me to describe the enormities committed. Great numbers are badly wounded, and much injury is otherwise sustained. I happened to be out of Coventry, but at my return ... at the risk of my own life, I went to the Barracks and requested the troops be immediately called in, with which request the officer ... complied.

Nothing came of this, but potentially it could easily have escalated in another Peterloo-style massacre. Men, woman and children cut down in the streets of Coventry by dragoons supporting their captain, who in turn, as a Whig candidate, was supported by the Corporation, and defended by the mayor.

The years 1806 and 1808 are interesting for the simple fact that Coventry elections for those years were considered to be 'quiet', as were a number of the following elections. However, chaos returned in 1820, the year the political writer William Cobbett joined the fray. He wrote: 'I was drawn through the principal streets ... on a frosty evening ... The acclamations were so general and so hearty ... the mass of people so clearly expressive of ardent attachment to the cause of which I was representative.' Cobbett continued: 'However, I resolved to proceed with caution.' He was right to do so, for soon after:

Our friends satisfied with the victory of the day had retired to their homes when the savages who had been hired by the band of rich ruffians sallied forth, dashed in the windows of the house of Mr Sergeant [in Earl Street], at which I was, and made many brutal attacks upon individuals who they took unawares in the streets or public houses. Even in this early period they cut several persons with knives, and there is no doubt in my mind that they were furnished with knives by their employers, for the express purpose of being used in cutting and stabbing ... the knives appear to have been all of one sort, or nearly so ---- stout pen-knives with sharp points. I saw two drunken savages, carter fellows, brandishing each a knife to rip my voters up.

Cobbett failed but again contested the seat in 1824, when his opponents were Moore and Ellice. Edward Ellice was to become a political giant in the city for years to come. Cobbett wrote in the *Political Register*:

I had to pass through a band of savages and I was scarcely amongst them when they (at Ellice's instigation) began to endeavour to press me down. They were more than a thousand in number ... several attempts were made to press me down. I got many blows in the sides, and if I had been either a short or weak man I must have been pressed under foot and inevitably killed ... with a great deal of difficulty I reached the pavement ... I had when I left the booth, my snuff box in my right hand. It is oblong and has very sharp corners, the savages pressed me sideways towards my left, and I had to fight with my right hand, in order to

William Cobbett, politican, journalist and writer, came very close to losing more than the election when he joined the fray.

In the 1832 election the King's Head was described as resembling a slaughterhouse. That election afterwards became known as the 'Bloody Tenth'.

prevent them from getting me down. It cut the noses and eyes of the savages at a furious rate and assisted in my safe arrival on the raised pavement ... just opposite the door of a shop.

To cries of 'hang him!' Cobbett was dragged to safety through the doorway of the shop by two women. He kicked one 'savage' between the eyes and sending him sprawling back into the frenzied mob. Cobbett later wrote, 'these poor fellows bear the name of Freeman and are all the while real slaves as are the Negroes in Jamaica.'

Cobbett came and went, but Ellice stayed. The 1832 election began with a huge mob escorting Ellice and Bulwer to the hustings. When their opponents Fyler and Thomas left the King's Head to go to the election booth they were assaulted. Neither could enter until they were assisted by 'specials'. In the days that followed they shipped in their own mob, made up of Birmingham pugilists and 600 navvies – all well oiled with 'gin-hot'. Clubs in hand they occupied the booth. Meanwhile, Ellice and Bulwer's mob, numbering around 3,000, gathered on Greyfriar's Green and armed themselves with clubs and staves. Bob Randle, a local prize-fighter, led the mob who marched on the booth. Randle exchanged words with the opposition, and threw a punch – and battle ensued. Randle's mob eventually won the day, leaving many stripped and beaten. Dozens fled back to the King's Head, which was described as resembling a slaughterhouse. This war was won by Bulwer and Ellice and thereafter became known as the 'Bloody Tenth'.

Things changed the following year when 1,000 special constables were sworn in and – amazingly – managed to hold the peace. Later, the Municipal Reform Act helped to put a halt to the violence by replacing corrupt closed Corporations with town councils. Now members of the council were not just elected by Freemen but by ratepayers, property owners. All helped to put an end to Coventry's violent elections. However, although election violence may have ended, corruption and bribery continued, albeit on a more limited scale, into the early twentieth century.

THE GREAT PRIZE FIGHTS

PRIZE FIGHTING – that is, fighting with bare fists for a purse – was a development from the stable of James Figg, a sword-master in the eighteenth century. Prize fighting in England was an extremely popular sport – or science, as proponents prefer to call it. In this era it even had its own slang: claret for blood; bread basket for face; peepers for eyes. The sport was favoured by all, from the richest to the poorest. These fights commanded large audiences: the more important the fight, the bigger the audience, 5,000 or 10,000 spectators not being an unusual number. The best views were taken by the wealthy, who usually sat in their own carriages (which encircled the ring). The 'Fancy', as they liked to be called, encircled the roped-off circle for the fight. Technically each prize fight was

An engraving of 'the Fancy', in their carriages, rushing to watch a prize fight (shown at the bottom).

illegal, and many fights were broken up by magistrates. Many, of course, were not, as those in charge turned a blind eye – indeed, they often attended themselves. Despite the illegality of the fights, their popularity meant that they had to be constantly reported in the press.

On 1 January 1813 the *Coventry Herald* reported on one such fight: 'The boxing match between John Bagshaw, and ----- Kettle, a labourer, both of this City.' It took place at Well's Green, near the road between Coventry and Birmingham. It lasted for fifty-two minutes, during which twenty-one rounds were fought – meaning twenty-one knockdowns. Kettle, the stronger of the two men, won the purse of 20 guineas. Interestingly, after the report of the fight the *Coventry Herald* adds:

> We must now express our astonishment that in this enlightened age, men are yet to be found who will engage to bruise and mangle each other until one of the combatants shall be declared unable to strike another blow. We have uniformly expressed our abhorrence of such brutal arrangements ... We cannot sufficiently applaud the conduct of those Magistrates who exerted themselves, and actually prevented the conflict taking place in this county.

Despite their condemnation of the sport, prize fighting was to grow and the *Herald*, like many other newspapers, would continue to report it for years to come. On 27 February 1829 the *Herald* reported on a colourful fight between 'the Flash Barber' and 'the Chicken Butcher':

> On Monday last an occasional turn up took place at the back of Hammerton's Mill [Longford], in this City, in consequence of an old grudge between Bill Hayfield, the Flash Barber, and Jack Hammerton, alias the Chicken Butcher. These two fistic heroes had twice entered the field before, and this was to decide who really was the best man ... The fight lasted half an hour ... [until] the Chicken Butcher ... cried, 'enough' amidst the deafening shouts of the friends of the victor.

On the same Monday, in the evening, a number of sparring matches took place at the Royal Oak, Gosford Street. The street was the heart of the Coventry Fancy and many of its pubs were connected and displayed regular bouts of fistic prowess within their walls. The first was between Jem Reading, the 'Living Skeleton', and the 'Cockney Dyer'. The second was between Ginger Berry and Bacon Smith; then John 'Fatty' Adrian fought against Trainer Walker. The fourth bout was between the 'Pride of the Wharf' – 'no doubt a bargee or a labourer from the canal wharf' – against the 'Ostler at the Crane', the stableman at the Crane Inn, in Bishop Street. Next up was a tussle between Strogger Russell and Buck Gutteridge, in which Buck apparently had 'no chance'. Bacon Smith then fought Lun Caldicott, and 'the former drew claret from the latter four times running'. Trainer Walker then took on Matthews the Plasterer, in a battle

The Royal Oak in Gosford Street. In the 1820s it was known as the heart of the 'Coventry Fancy'. Here many tournament bouts were held.

said to have been a beautiful display of the science. This was followed by Long-Waist Gilbert against Trainer Walker – who, being tired from the previous round against Fatty Adrian, promptly lost. The Skeleton then took on Young Tip. The night ended with Peter Smith, alias Come-by-night, challenging any man in the room for £20.

In a field near Kenilworth in March 1829, another grand battle took place. Bob Randall, a young man from Nuneaton, took on John Fatty Adrian, a noted fighter who resided in Much Park Street. The fight was again reported by the *Herald*:

The place of fighting was not decided till Monday afternoon ... Coventry disgorged its hundreds and Birmingham, Warwick, Nuneaton, &c, &c, their thousands ... early on Tuesday

morning the F.P.C.S. were pitched in good order, attended by a number of able-bodied individuals to preserve the outer ring, with long whips which they did not spare the use of ... Beside the outer ring ... there were waggons, carts and vehicles of every description ... amongst the vast mass, were people of all ranks and degrees; the rich and the poor ...

... Randall was led into the ring by the Commissary General and Perkins the Oxford Pet ... he was received with deafening shouts of applause; and as soon as he arrived at the ropes he hurled his castor [gauntlet] inside and entered ... Adrian was quick at his heels attended by his trainer, Walker, and Hawkes his second ... He was also loudly cheered ... On stripping Bob had the appearance of anything but a 'fighting cove' – he looked like a modest, serious, pale-faced young man ... Fatty on the other hand, looked as tho' he meant to win. At length the awful, long looked for moment arrived ... a pin might now have been heard to drop; as soon as they were placed the seconds withdrew a short distance, and to it they went.

Round one: Fatty went down; two, Randall fell; three, Fatty fell 'like a Bullock'; four, Randall was thrown out of the ropes. In the eleventh, another 'stomacher' for Adrian and a 'facer' for Randall. In the fourteenth and fifteenth, both went down together. Round twenty-five: 'time was called. Poor Fatty was deaf, and his seconds hurled the sponge into the air.' The *Herald* continues:

This fight, which lasted 37 minutes, was one of the best ever witnessed in this part of the country ... poor Fatty could not recover himself at all, and when the battle was over, he was obliged to be held by one of his seconds, while he sat on the other's knee. He was bled on the ground and carried off senseless, but was well enough to appear the same night at the White Lion, in this City.

At the end of March 1829 two fights took place on Whitley Common for £2 a side between Bill Hayfield and Bob Smith. The fight lasted an hour and a half, during which fifty-nine rounds were fought, and it ended in favour of Hayfield. This was followed by a match between Bacon Smith and Peter Smith, 'during which seven such desperate rounds were fought as are seldom witnessed by the admirers of the science. Bacon proved the victor.'

In November 1830 Adrian took on Bill Betteridge for 40 sovereigns in a field by the Engine public house in Longford. The betting was initially in favour of Adrian – though Betteridge, it was said, had a crooked arm, which he called his 'vice'. This he used to lock his opponent's head so he could punch them. He was several inches taller than Adrian, heavier and stronger, and by the third and fourth round betting had turned towards Betteridge. The *Herald* reported:

Jack [John] gave the first knockdown blow, and showed himself decidedly the best fighter, placing at least half a dozen blows to his opponent's one. Betteridge drew first blood; during the fight, he more than once got his 'vice' around Adrian's neck ... Although fighting up hill, Adrian's game supported him through 105 punishing rounds, which lasted about 2¾ hours.

The fight, however, was prematurely ended when the 'beaks' turned up and broke it up. Still illegal, fights

A prize fight in the 1830s, from a print by Alken.

took place in remote places and on county borders so those involved could jump counties and thus avoid the county sheriffs.

A rematch was held the following year on 5 April 1831 in a field near Fillongley before 5,000 spectators; the prize was £100. Betteridge, however, won the day.

John Adrian was an interesting example of a Coventry prize fighter. Born in Gosford Street in 1806, the descendant of a Walsgrave vicar, he was apprenticed to his father, a master weaver, and in 1828 was made a Freeman of the city. By 1830, with his early winnings, he had acquired The Windmill in Spon Street; he later held the Leopard Inn in Smithford Street, and lastly the Pitt's Head in Far Gosford Street (a noted prize fighter's pub). Fatty Adrian was not a fat man: he earned his name at a fair in Coventry, where he had successfully climbed a 'fatted pole' (i.e. a pole covered in grease) and won a suckling pig. After this victory, which left him covered in goose fat, his friends began to call him Fatty. Fatty Adrian died on 12 December 1856, at the age of fifty, in his home in Cook Street, from bronchitis and injured ribs, injuries which he had sustained in his prize-fighting days.

In October 1831 a fight took place on Whitley Common between Ginger Berry and Harry Hodson of Longford for 5 sovereigns a piece. In the first round Ginger struck Hodson under the right ear and laid him out. The seconds were unable to get him back to the scratch mark (from where the fighters stood toe to toe, hence the

Smithford Street in the 1860s, just a few years after Fatty Adrian died. The Leopard Inn, just one of his businesses, was here.

saying 'come up to scratch'), and Ginger was declared the victor without having received a single blow. Ginger Berry was fast gaining a reputation as a handy fighter, and afterwards looked to take on Betteridge for £100.

In December 1836, two Coventry pugilists, 'Game One' Shilton and 'Whopper' Flint, fought on Whitley Common, 'not far from the spot where the malefactors are hanged'. Due to the interest of local magistrates the site was kept secret. On the morning of the fight the crowds headed for Warwick, but the magistrates of that town broke the crowd up. Later in the day the 'respectable company' quietly set up a ring on Whitley Common and the fight commenced. After twenty-three rounds, Shilton was declared the victor.

Coventry's most noted fighter was William 'Paddy' Gill, born in Dublin in 1820. Gill came to Coventry at the age of five and was apprenticed to a ribbon weaver in Whitefriars Street. He completed his apprenticeship and was made a Freeman of Coventry in St Mary's Hall. At this time he was frequenting the Sword & Mace in Earl Street, a prize fighter's pub, where his first bouts caught the eye of the landlord, local sporting legend William King. King trained him up and set up his first fights. Later King recalled how Gill 'bruised over some local nobodies and was pitted against a big fellow named Foster, who he disposed of in a rattling fight.'

Paddy's first fight for a purse was set up by King in 1838 on Radford Common against local fighter Bill Heap for £5 each. Heap fought well but Paddy proved the victor, battling his way

Paddy Gill was Coventry's greatest prize fighter, and gained national prominence.

through fifty-five hard-fought rounds. The more he fought, the greater grew his repute – and the fight's purse. In November 1842 he took on Hubbard of Nuneaton for £25 per fighter. This battle proved a draw, but at the rematch – which William King states took place in deep snow nearly up to the men's fighting breeches – Paddy 'knocked the buckram out of Hubbard. That wor' a day an no' mistake.'

By October 1843 Paddy had moved to a higher league, taking on national fighter Norley of Manchester for £50 a side. This bruising match lasted one hour and fifty-five minutes, and Paddy lost. He did, however, win his next three fights, quickly finding himself back in the top league. He was matched against London bruiser Reed 'the Invincible'. Invincible, however, he wasn't, and Paddy proved the victor, taking the huge purse of £200. He then fought Norley in a rematch on Tuesday, 12 May 1846, for a massive purse of £500 (roughly £66,000 today). The match was fought at Whitney in Oxfordshire and lasted four hours and fifteen minutes. The fight lasted for 160 rounds – meaning that between them they were beaten to the ground 160 times.

A broadside at the time consists of a song celebrating the fight:

On the hundredth round these heroes met, when Paddy did let fly.
And with his left a stunning hit, caught Norley in the eye;
The same dose he did repeat, which made his head to ring.
The Coventry lads cried, 'Norley, your canaries will not sing.'

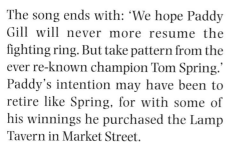

DEATH BY HORSE: THE TRAGIC END OF ANOTHER COVENTRY SPORT

Boxing was not the only sport which brought tragedy to Coventry. In September 1783 an unusual accident took place which brought an end to horse racing in the Coventry Great Park. On a Tuesday, Sir John Shelley's bay horse, Lofty, won the Member's Plate and £30. The following day Shelley's other horse, a chestnut called Eclipse, won the Subscription Plate and £50. The races were hugely attended with many gentry in the grounds, including Lord Sheffield and Lady Herbert. There was a ball each evening in Draper's Hall and on Thursday the gentry left. The races after this were smaller events. On Thursday a race for a silver cup was won by a Coventry butcher, and a small child met a strange and untimely end.

The *Mercury* reported:

> This day's avocation was attended by a melancholy accident, for one of the horses running away with his rider, made directly for the Gate leading from the Park into Little-park-street, and some persons endeavouring to hinder him from going through the gate, which was open, he leapt over the turn-stile by the side of it, fell upon a fine girl about 7 years of age, and killed her on the spot.

Racing resumed again many years later in Stoke and Radford.

The song ends with: 'We hope Paddy Gill will never more resume the fighting ring. But take pattern from the ever re-known champion Tom Spring.' Paddy's intention may have been to retire like Spring, for with some of his winnings he purchased the Lamp Tavern in Market Street.

In 1848, however, the lure of the ring proved too great: he took on the notorious Tom Maley in London and again walked, or maybe staggered, away with the purse. Paddy was now seen as a national champion, with incredible strength, stamina and endurance, but in 1850 it all went tragically wrong. On 27 July that year Paddy was matched to Thomas Griffiths at Frimley Green. The two fought a hard battle when suddenly, with one blow to the head, Griffiths was felled – only this time he did not get up. Paddy had killed his opponent.

The following April Paddy was put on trial for manslaughter. The close circle of the prize ring protected their man: no one could be found who would place Paddy at the scene, so he walked free. However, though he may have been free in his body, Paddy was troubled in his mind; he withdrew from the ring and concentrated his efforts on running the Lamp. Life did not end well for Coventry's greatest fighter: Paddy began to suffer from mental problems, no doubt due to the thousands of punches his brain had absorbed. He was eventually put in Hatton Asylum, near Warwick, where one day he literally fell down dead while walking the grounds. Paddy Gill was fifty years old when, in 1869, his body was brought back to Coventry, to the London Road Cemetery, where he was buried as a famous exemplar of the pugilistic art. His grave lies there still, amongst this garden of the dead, uncared for and overgrown.

THE END?

It is generally assumed that the prize ring disappeared with the introduction of the Marquis of Queensbury's Rules, brought in by an aristocrat of that title and specifying new guidelines such as 'no wrestling or hugging (clinching) allowed', 'a man hanging on the ropes in a helpless state, with his toes off the ground, shall be considered down' and 'a man on one knee is considered down and if struck is entitled to the stakes'.

This is, however, untrue. The *Coventry Herald* of 18 December 1881 reported on another boxing manslaughter trial:

> The trial of the nine men charged with manslaughter in connection with the fatal prize-fight on Hearsall Common took place at the Warwick Assizes yesterday. [The judge said] ... a number of people appear to have encouraged two wretched men to beat each other as nearly as possible to death. In the present case the two men fought several rounds until at last one of them was clearly beaten and should have given in ... But with the instinct of his race the defeated man would not yield, and the result that he was beaten to death by his opponent.

Although this sounds like an account of an ordinary fight, a second report smacks more of the old prize ring, police interference included, but not the massive crowds. It states:

> Arnold's opponent, a man named Plant, was hurt so badly that he died the next day, and Arnold was indicted for manslaughter and sentenced to six months' imprisonment. The men, with their supporters and others, first met in what was then familiarly known as Wyley's Field, off the London Road [Charterhouse], and then went to Whitley Common. At Whitley Common a police sergeant interfered, and the Park, but later rejoined on Hearsall Common, where the fight took place, lasting three quarters of an hour. After the first few rounds Plant was out-classed, but showed plenty of pluck to the end, this characteristic being remarked on by the judge at the trial. In the evening he became insensible, and died ... the post mortem examination showed, besides serious injuries to the head and other parts of the body, [a] fracture of the nose and several ribs.

John 'Jacco' Plant met his fate before a small crowd of seventy people. His opponent, Samuel Arnold, was given six months' hard labour. Plant's funeral was attended by 3,000 people. The days of Georgian-style prize fighting had finally ended.

AD 1831

THE WEAVERS' RIOT

IN THE REIGN of William IV, Coventry suffered one of the most violent riots in British history. This, however, was nothing new: the city has a long history of tumult and unrest. In 1756, for example, Bedworth's colliers attacked Coventry. The city was forced to defend itself: 'city constables and specials were sworn in and brought the troubles to an end, armed to the teeth with bludgeons and cutlasses.' As this chapter will show, this was not to be the last of it: Bedworth colliers – along with many of the other trades – would bring riot back to the city time and time again.

John Hewitson, of Coventry Archives, unearthed the following story of another of the city's melees. Friday, 26 September 1766, in the Women's Market (or by the Coventry Cross in Cross Cheaping), saw Coventry Cheese Fair, one of the largest cheese fairs in the county, in full swing. Coventry and Warwickshire cheeses produced on local farms were, in the past, noted throughout the nation for their richness and quality. Into this scene marched 200 Bedworth miners, armed with pick-axe handles. They were here to protest against the rising price of cheese (which, with bread, was the mainstay of the eighteenth-century worker's diet).

This hike in prices was often caused by London merchants buying up Warwickshire cheeses for the London market. This helped to cause a shortage locally as the local makers hoarded cheeses in their warehouses, letting it out bit by bit at a greatly enhanced price. Magistrates thought they had tackled the problem by banning London cheese merchants from buying locally, but the merchants helped the problem to remain.

Bishop Street in the late nineteenth century. In September 1800, 2,000 Bedworth miners marched down here on Coventry.

The miners, who were a law unto themselves, decided to sort this out and marched into Coventry on market day. They went to the warehouses of two Coventry cheese merchants which held hoarded cheese, broke the locks and loaded the cheese on waggons. Then took it into the market and began to sell at the old price of two and a half pence a pound for the mature and two pence for new cheese. They then returned the money they had taken to the merchants who owned the cheese, thereby avoiding legal action.

In September 1800 the miners and others were back, 2,000 of them marching on Coventry to try to force down the price of flour, bread and cheese, which had risen greatly in price. The huge crowd marched into Bishop Street – only to be confronted by the mayor and a number of troops blocking the way. The mayor tried to calm the mob, but was threatened with death if he didn't sign a document to the effect that prices were to be reduced. Stones were thrown and the mayor read the Riot Act, sending forth the 17th Regiment of the Light Dragoons to disperse the crowd. Some of the rioters, however, broke into the city through the back streets and raided the shops which sold at exaggerated prices; these were also soon after dispersed. Later the mayor set up the 'Committee for Bettering the Condition of the Poor' to purchase and sell flour, bread, cheese and vegetables from the top of Butcher Row at a reduced price to the poor. This seemed to satisfy the Bedworth miners – or 'Black Tribe', as they were then known.

Real riots broke out three decades later, in 1829, as the *Coventry Herald* reported on 15 May:

We are sorry to have to record any ebullition of unpleasant feeling in Coventry, but the public mind was considerably alarmed on Saturday evening last [14th], in consequence of a crowd of persons who had collected in Broad Gate. The first symptom of riot and disorder commenced about five o'clock, by parcels of youths creating disturbances, &c., and at length they went up to a man named Watson, who had a quantity of potatoes on sale, for which he was asking 6d per gallon, and the crowd began to abuse him and say that he had bought them that morning at 3d a gallon and now he wanted to sell them for 6d. They insisted that he should do no such thing, and began to use threats and intimidations to him, and we believe, succeeded in making him sell at a reduced price.

At this point Mr Carter, the constable, came up, and took a youth who appeared to be the leader into custody. He was taken to the watch house, but as there was no magistrate's order the keeper refused to take him in. The *Herald* continues:

We have no hesitation to say, that had the constables done their duty then, and apprehended the principal aggressors, peace would have been restored in a few minutes, there being at that time not above fifty individuals in the crowd. But finding their companion at liberty, it gave them encouragement to go on, and then

COVENTRY'S DEADLIEST FOOD!

It wasn't just cheese that was causing chaos in historical Coventry. The *Midland Daily Telegraph* of January 1896 reported an unlucky fruit-related death: 'The death occurred on Wednesday, at High Fields, Payne's Lane, of Thos Stokes, a native of Coventry, but until recently engaged at Woolwich Arsenal. On 26 December Stokes slipped on a piece of orange peel in King William Street. He was picked up by a boy named Edward Redding, with his head badly cut, and was taken to hospital. He was under treatment there a short time, attended as an out-patient, but never recovered from the effects of the fall, and died as stated.'

proceeded to all the potato standings in the market. By this time the crowd had considerably augmented, and they proceeded down Butcher Row, to the different butcher's shops compelling them to sell their meat two pence and three pence per lb., under their regular prices; from the Butcher Row they returned to Broad Gate.

At this instance Alderman Vale came up, and placing himself in the doorway of Mr Goodman's [butcher's] shop prevented the mischief that would have otherwise followed; as Mr Goodman was prepared with a large knife and his men with other defensive weapons … At this juncture, the Mayor and other magistrates began to assemble, and all the ward constables, with the watchmen, &c. &c. were summoned to the Police Office; and just at that moment, a Troop of the 14th Light Dragoons, which had left here in the morning on route to Leeds, returned.

Things quickly calmed down and by 10 p.m. all was quiet. The following day, Sunday, passed without incident,

mainly because a company of the 93rd Highlanders marched into the city to assist in holding the peace.

On Monday, however, small groups of weavers gathered. Some burned an effigy of a ribbon manufacturer and committed other 'mischiefs', including threats and intimidation. The chief magistrate of the city spoke to them a number of times asking them to respect other people and conceded to their request to hold a general meeting, which was held in the afternoon, when 3,000 weavers gathered on Greyfriar's

In the 1829 riot the mob forced the butchers of Butcher's Row to sell their meat at lower prices.

Green. The weavers worries about the trade were placated – but not for long. The scene was set for one of Coventry's greatest riots.

THE RIOT BEGINS

On 7 November 1831 the fuse was lit. It was reported that: 'a riot of Considerable Magnitude took place and the Rioters not only attacked a house in the occupation of a Mr Josiah Beck, a manufacturer of looms for the weaving of Ribbons, but destroyed all the looms and Machinery in it, and then set fire to the house, which was burned to the ground in the parish of Holy Trinity.'

In the lead up to this riot the weaving trade in Coventry had been in a depressed state. This meant that many of the weaving masters had dropped the amount a weaver (many of whom worked from home) could get for his finished cloth. Naturally, the weavers weren't very happy about this. On the day in question a large number of weavers had gathered to discuss the problem. By 3 p.m. weavers numbering between 400 and 500 people had gathered at Cross Cheaping where, after much agitation regarding falling wages and the new-fangled steam loom, 200 of the group decided to march on the premises of ribbon and loom manufacturer Josiah Beck. The 'manufactory', which stood at the end of Beck's Yard in New Buildings, was of no great size: three stories high, it contained a small number of looms including eight which were steam-powered, most of which were still under construction. This was the real complaint of the weavers: the introduction of multi-production steam-powered looms – the robots of their age – had meant unemployment for many, and possibly starvation for some.

When the group reached the manufactory, they banged on the door; Beck – shouting through the door – asked what they wanted. To see the

---

MELANCHOLY DEATHS OF TWO COVENTRY COLLIERS

In November 1830 bones were discovered in Wyken Colliery, which stood behind Eburne School on Deedmore Road. Said the *Herald*:

On the 26th May 1810, the roof of a pit at this colliery gave way, and a quantity of water and earth rushing in, it was almost immediately filled up. The hands at work in the pit made their escape, with the exception of John Millerchip, aged 24, and Samuel Randle, aged 17, who unfortunately perished. On Saturday last, while some men were getting coals in a pit lately sunk near the one in which the accident happened, the bones of the above individuals were discovered, and every exertion being made, on Monday last the entire skeletons of each were found. Mr Harris the agent of the works, had them placed in a coffin, and on the following day they were interred.

---

machinery, they replied. Beck opened the door. He saw Joseph Day, one of the ringleaders, who he knew, and agreed to let him enter. Day stepped forward – and as Beck stood aside to let him pass the mob surged in, pushing him out of the way. Beck's servant slammed the door shut but Beck was trapped outside. Almost immediately, he was stoned with bricks and coal. He took quite a beating before he managed to clamber up a wall, struggling desperately to escape. Sadly, however, it was not to be – before he could get over the wall and away to safety he was caught. A weaver called John Deeming, with several others, dragged him back to the factory and forced him to open the steam-engine room. As the mob set about the factory, Beck escaped again – but was again recaptured. He was thrown into a hand cart and wheeled into Ironmonger Row, where he was thrown into some mud. After he got up, he was pulled towards Mr Ladbury's house. Mr Ladbury was stunned when he saw the bleeding factory owner.

'What's this?' he said. 'We'll have to get you into the house before you are killed!'

Before the pair could move, however, Beck received a blow on the head which knocked him senseless to the ground. Semi-conscious, he was dragged off, like a rag doll, pushed and pulled by the mob who took him back to the factory. There the main door remained locked against them. The mob insisted that he should open the door, or they would kill him. Beck was forced to shout to his servants inside, and eventually the door was opened. Then the situation took a turn for the worse.

'Now, you bastard, I'll make you destroy your own inventions!' one rioter told his employer. Then the mob rushed in.

Beck again tried to flee, dashing into an entry where he was taken by more of the mob. He was struck three or four further times. The crowd started to shout – 'duck him!' – as he struggled free and stumbled onwards. He hid under a dresser in a nearby house, but the mob soon found him, so he ran into Moy's Timber Yard – where a horrible sight awaited him. Flames reached upwards – his factory was ablaze.

As he stared, the mob once again caught up with him. He was dragged to the Mill Dam Pool. Here he was surrounded by a group of baying weavers, who struck at him and threatened to kill him. Beck took a hard punch and, kneeling on the ground, started to plead for his life. As weaver John Bascett later remembered in court, '[I] saw Beck kneeling down, holding up his hands; did not hear

An early nineteenth-century engraving of the Mill Dam, which lay roughly in the area in front of the Transport Museum. Here James Beck was dragged during the Beck Riot.

anyone swear at Beck ... some of the people were hissing and cried shame while others said it served Beck right.'

One Thomas Burbury – who apparently had earlier called for the factory to be put to the flame – intervened at this point and talked the mob out of any final act of violence. He helped Beck to his feet and led him away from the danger.

Meanwhile, the mob was on the rampage. They rushed through Beck's factory smashing windows, looms and steam engines. The *Coventry Herald & Observer* reported:

In about a quarter of an hour from the time of the attack the factory was found to be on fire, and in less than 20 minutes, owing to the quantity of dry wood being on the premises, the flames rushed from all the windows of the house, the roof was soon seen to fall in, and by four o'clock the fire had reduced the whole to ruins. A man named Wood, who had been employed in the factory, narrowly escaped being burned to death. When the attack was first made, he ran upstairs to the garret where he concealed himself behind some reels. The fire however reached him, the boards on the floor were burning under his feet, and there was no alternative but to perish in the flames, or descend from the window. He accordingly took a blanket from off a bed in the room, fastened it inside, and fortunately let himself down without sustaining any injury.

Some additional information may be found in Coventry's archives:

On the news reaching the Police Office, the Magistrates were promptly in attendance, and Messrs. Aldermen Weare, Douglas and Rotherham hastened to the spot where the Riot Act was immediately read ... The crowd which was now considerable began to disperse. A party of the 14th Light Dragoons, and another of the 7th Hussars, stationed here, were immediately called out ... they proceeded direct to the scene of action, dispersed the mob, and leaving sufficient guard over the property, commenced clearing the streets. The shops were closed and the City at this time presented altogether an alarming aspect.

... A handbill was issued by the Magistrates, calling on the respectable inhabitants to attend and act as special constables. The invitation was complied with, and many of the most respectable men in the City were sworn in. The theatre and public houses were closed. Soldiers were stationed in and near the premises of Messrs. Day and Dodd, ribbon manufacturers, residing in Gosford-street, against whom much indignation was felt by the weavers, owing to their having given out work at a very reduced price ... By twelve o'clock at night all was quiet, and has since continued so. As a precautionary measure, the military and special constables patrolled during the night.

By the morning Beck's factory was a smouldering, burnt-out shell. Raids were carried out overnight and a small group of men arrested, including William Westwick, Joseph Day and Benjamin Sparkes. The somewhat ironically named Alfred Toogood was

CITY of COVENTRY.

Whereas,

TUMULTUOUS

ASSEMBLIES

OF PERSONS

HAVE THIS DAY TAKEN PLACE IN THIS CITY,

AND

Tumult & Riot are Apprehended,

The Mayor & Magistrates

Of this City hereby Order and Direct every Licensed Victualler, and every Person Licensed to Sell Beer by Retail, within the said City and Suburbs, to

Close their respective Houses,

At the Hour of   in the   of this Day, pursuant to the Statutes in such Case made and provided.---Dated the   day of   183

GEORGE ELD,

MAYOR.

Police Office,

HENRY MERRIDEW, PRINTER, SMITHFORD-STREET, COVENTRY.

A Riot Bill closed inns and taverns, to stop drink fuelling disorder. Printed in 1835, under the mayoralty of George Eld, it was always ready to be filled in at the appropriate time.

arrested the following day and, on the Wednesday, so was Thomas Burbury, Beck's rescuer.

THE TRIAL

Most of the men were eventually released for lack of evidence. Four only remained: Burbury, Toogood, Sparkes, and one John Deeming.

They were placed on trial for unlawful, riotous and tumultuous assembly. Deeming was found not guilty, and Toogood was judged to have been 'led on' by the others and recommended a sentence of transportation – but Burbury and Sparkes were found guilty of all charges. The judge therefore placed the black cap on his head and pronounced the death sentence: 'That you be taken back to the prison from whence you came, and that you be taken from thence to a place of execution, and that you there be hanged by the neck until you are dead.'

Coventry was in shock: two of its citizens were to be executed. Petitions were signed by MPs Edward Ellice and Henry Bulwer – even Beck himself signed. At the last minute the death sentences were transmuted to transportation, Burbury's reprieve arriving only the day before his execution was due to take place. In 1832 the three were transported to Tasmania. Burbury was pardoned in 1837, and later became a field police constable. When he died he left a large house surrounded by groves. His son William, who inherited his estate, bought other properties, increasing the estate further to 50,000 acres. His son Stanley became Sir Stanley Burbury, governor of Tasmania.

The *Coventry Standard* reported in later years: 'There died on the 7th Oct 1876, one of the almsmen of Bond's or Bablake Hospital, at the advanced age of 84 years ---- Josiah Beck, an old man ... in his early days a clever and ingenious mechanic.'

Newspapers noted that Toogood was still in Australia, 'a respectable man and doing well'. Ironically, the introducer of the steam loom to Coventry fared the worst – because of other people's actions, Beck died a pauper.

CHRISTMAS CATASTROPHES

BOILED IN HIS OWN BEER!

The year 1899 was an unusual year for unusual deaths. The first was of thirty-five-year-old George Rainbow, the landlord of the Admiral Codrington Inn in St Nicholas Street. At an inquest, held in the Old Mayoress's Parlour in St Mary's Hall, Rainbow's wife gave her evidence. 'On Wednesday morning [13th December],' she told the court:

> ...he went, at half past eight, to the brewhouse to commence brewing operations. He completed the preliminary work, and then went into the city to transact some business. When he came back he went into the brewhouse and returned saying, 'It's all right,' and conversed with several customers in the house. He knew when the water in the vat was boiling, and ready for use. Deceased was not subject to fits, and she had never known him become faint or giddy. He was perfectly sober at the time he commenced mashing. There was always a stool by the side of the copper; the latter was encased in brickwork. The height of the copper from the floor was such that she could not see into it. She considered it would be about six feet high.

You may be able to guess what happened next. It appears that Rainbow was in the habit of standing on a stool on a beer crate to work this vat. His wife testified that she was 'in the yard ... when she heard the deceased call out'.

She cried, 'Oh! What have you done?'

Her husband replied, 'Oh, Liz, save me!'

She saw him on the side of the copper struggling to get out. She believed he had fallen in backwards. She assisted in getting him out of the copper, where he freely observed the accident 'is my death blow'. When out of the copper it was seen that he was dreadfully scalded. When his clothes were taken off him, the skin came off too. Dr Day said that the deceased died from 'shock to the system' at about 10.30 p.m.

If anything appalling crops up, observed the coroner as he recorded this judgement, 'it is always around

The Admiral Codrington in St Nicholas Street, where George Rainbow, the landlord, met his unfortunate fate.

Christmas time'. How true that remark was to prove to be – for on Christmas Day of that same year a double fatality occurred.

CHOKED AT COVENTRY CROSS CYCLE COMPANY!

The *Midland Daily Telegraph* reported on two men who were 'found suffocated on the premises of the Coventry Cross Cycle Company, Foleshill Road. The firm required some alterations in regard to their boilers and the Dowson Gas Company sent down from London, to effect the repairs, two men, whose full names and addresses are at present unknown.'

It seems that the cycle firm's gas holder was by the canal. The structure had slipped, causing some damage, and as the works was closed on Christmas Day it was thought to be a good time to carry out the repairs.

Mr W. Glanville attended the works on Christmas morning and had a chat with the men, who were then busy at their work. This was the last time he would see them alive. On the evening of the following night he was summoned back to the works, and 'the sight he there witnessed was a very startling one. Inside the gas holder were the two men mentioned, stiff and dead ... when the bodies were brought out of the gasometer it was at once seen that human help was unavailable as life was extinct. One man was about

42 years of age and the other about 32 years of age.'

BAKED IN HIS OWN OVEN!

Four days later, a third horrifying incident happened to a young baker called Frank Morris. Frank, a master baker, worked at a bakery in a yard between Nos 55 and 54 Smithford Street. He had been seen by several people that day and was working as normal. At one o'clock a friend saw him in the bake house, and said a parting word, 'so long', for which he received a cheerful response. Shortly afterwards he appears to have gone missing. A boy who assisted him spent an hour searching for his master before he found him. As the *Midland Daily Telegraph* reported:

> At about half past three the lad secured entrance to the bake house, which appears to have been locked from the inside. The boy was going to put some water in the oven when he saw the feet of what proved to be the remains of his master. He at once called for assistance, and the dead body was pulled out of the oven. The body was considerably burned, and it seemed likely that the young man had been inside the oven for some time. As to how he got there is unknown. The police were fetched, and the remains were conveyed to the infirmary in the Workhouse.
>
> ...Further particulars go to show that the body was charred in a fearful manner. Both Morris's hands had practically dropped off, hanging only by a little flesh. The flesh on one of the arms had fallen away from the bone, whilst the face is described as being as black as ink, and the eyes had sunk in. The man was fully dressed, and his clothing was scorched. The oven is about breast high, so that it seems impossible that the man could have fallen inside. When the discovery was made the fires on either side had died out about an hour, although the oven itself was sufficiently hot to bake bread at the time. In the bake house there was a quantity of dough which the deceased had prepared some hours previously in readiness for baking ... Morris, who was a member of the Master Bakers' Association, was about 27 years of age. He lived at 14, Spencer Street with his parents. He was unmarried.

DEADLY SHERBOURNE

Watery Disasters and the Great Flood

COVENTRY'S RIVER HAS a long history of causing death and devastation. Between 15 and 16 November 1770, as one report states, 'a mass of water rolled through the town with noise, violence and rapidity.' Goods were washed away, as were people; some residents, especially those living in cellars, were drowned. At one point it was even thought the very existence of the city was threatened – by the end of the deluge, the number of persons missing or drowned was said to be seventy-nine. However, nineteeth-century historian and schoolmaster William George Fretton noted that the number of burials recorded in church records only amounts to twenty-five, a reasonable average for this time of year. He suggested, therefore, that the report was a fabrication. (This may not be the case, but we can assume that the number of deaths in it is, at least, strongly exaggerated.)

On 9 November 1800 the Sherbourne again burst its banks, causing a general flood to reach parts never before reached. On 1 August 1834 the *Coventry Herald & Observer* reported another disaster:

During the present week, and particularly on Sunday last, this City, and neighbourhood cities, has been visited by several tremendous storms of thunder, lightning, wind and rain. In the course of one of these hurricanes, a stone was forced from some part of the steeple of St Michael's church, which in its fall knocked out the keystone and several others of an arched doorway below. Many of the streets were flooded, though we are not

The River Sherbourne passing under St George's Chapel in Gosford Street in the early nineteenth century. The Sherbourne and the Radford Brook were the main water sources in the city.

aware of any material damage being done within the city.

On the same day, Kenilworth lay underneath 3ft of water, and haystacks nearby stood in 4ft of water. 'La Mare' – the great lake that historically lay to the south of the castle – had re-emerged as the land re-flooded. Leamington was impassable; the road to Warwick impassable. In Warwick itself furniture from the first floor of a house floated into the street. Within a week of these events, however, the weather changed: temperatures were being recorded as 84 degrees in the shade and 118 in the sun.

The flood of 11 November 1852 was also severe. Many residents were made homeless, which prompted the setting up of a fund to help its victims. Coventry also saw floods in 1853, 1862, 1875 and 1883. On 8 June 1892, as the *Coventry Times* reported, another downpour struck:

About noon on Sunday an exceedingly heavy thunderstorm, accompanied by flashes of lightning, and a terrific downpour of rain and hail, broke over Coventry. One flash in particular caused great alarm ... People in some of the churches describe the sensation as being as though the edifices were shaken. At St John's the lightning was immediately followed by a pouring in of water from the roof ... In Stoney Stanton Road the house of Mr P. Curtis, baker, was struck by the lightning. The electric fluid ran through the roof of a bedroom ... disturbing the ridge tiles and slates, and splintering the cross beams and rafters. It also dislodged the grate in the bedroom and entered the kitchen below, affected a daughter of Mr Curtis's, rendering her insensible for some time, and temporarily taking away the use of the limbs.

On Mr Hollick's farm at Little Heath the lightning struck an elm tree, and killed five sheep that were lying at the foot of the tree near an iron hurdle.

A serious incident connected with the storm was that in a house occupied by Mr Hill, 5, Cherry Row, Weston Street three people were struck by lightning. At 12.30 on Sunday the family were in the house, Mr Hill being seated on the sofa, Mrs Hill standing in the middle of the room, and Mr John Hill seated in the armchair near the wall. Suddenly Mr John Hill seemed to be enveloped in flame, and Mrs Hill was thrown violently to the floor. Miss Hill, who was in the adjoining room, was turned round as though by a strong wind. Mr Hill called to his son to assist in raising his mother, but receiving no reply, he saw that he was unconscious, that his legs were thrown out, and that his body was rigid. He gradually regained consciousness, but as he did not open his eyes, it was though he had been struck blind ... the house itself presents a peculiar appearance. The fluid seems to have struck the chimney stack first, dislodged a number of tiles and then made a hole through the wall into the bedroom. Here it struck a picture which had been suspended by a wire, but the wire has disappeared. A large quantity of plaster has also been stripped off the walls and several other pictures scorched. The lightning also struck an iron bedstead and entered the room below by means of the two posts. In the kitchen nearly all the pictures show traces of the passage of the electric fluid, and there are holes in several parts of the ceiling and walls.

Back to the floods! The last of any note began in the dying hours of 31 December 1900. After a night of heavy rain the Sherbourne burst its banks and overflowed by the bridge in Cox Street, then spilling into Godiva Street and Ford Street. It surged forward carrying rubbish, wood, furniture and – even a chicken coop, still containing its chickens. Pool Meadow filled up, followed by the Smithfield Market and Hales Street. Rubbish blocked the bridges causing a backwash of water which flowed into Smithford Street and Fleet Street filling the interior of the church of St John the Baptist to the depth of 6ft. The marker still exists today.

The water continued to flow, taking in Queen Victoria Road, Croft Road and inundating Spon End. Hundreds of homes were flooded and rumours spread of a large number drowned,

1 January 1901: Godiva Street. It needs to be remembered that on the previous night the water level was nearer the height of the lamppost on the right.

though in truth only a couple of men drowned, one an elderly labourer from a court in Hill Street. The man was rescued by two council workers with a horse and cart, but by the time he was pulled from the water he was dead. The other main casualties were dogs, cats, pet rabbits, chickens and two goats.

Beryl Clarke shared the memories of her aunt, May, from the night the flood struck:

Feeling in some uncanny way that something was happening, I got out of bed to look through the window, which was three stories from the ground, and what I saw I could hardly believe, for our street was a river!!! I ran down to wake Gran and Beatrice.

Before morning the water reached high enough for us to touch it from the second-floor window. Gran made us all kneel down by the bed and say prayers, for she said we might all drown. I watched in the semi-darkness, for all the street lights had gone out. As I watched I saw what I thought was a body being brought towards us by the water, when suddenly it got caught on a top spike of a street gas lamp and burst. It was a huge bag of soot washed out of the chimney sweep's back yard!! It was such a relief – we all laughed a lot.

Our butcher, who lived in the next street, remembered his horse was fastened in the stable, but the water was pretty high by then and though the brave fellow swam to open the door and free the animal, it was so scared it plunged to get out and caused the door to close – and shut poor Mr Hewitt inside. He was drowned and the horse was found later quite safe on higher ground.

Above *1 January 1901: Queen Victoria Road under water.*

Left *1 January 1901: Smithford Street under water.*

...A sorry sight met Mum and Dad when they returned from Birmingham: everything downstairs was ruined, including stock my mother had stored in readiness to open a draper's store in the New Year. We were insured against fire but not flood! The river which ran through Coventry had overflowed through excessive rain. How well I remember New Year's Day 1901; we were all so hungry, and the tantalising way food in plenty kept swimming past us on the stairs. Armed with walking sticks we were trying to reach the dishes of food washed out of the larder, and only succeeded in sending them swirling away or capsizing into the dirty water.

Forty-eight hours after the flood had gone out of the house our iron-framed piano was on its back at the opposite side of the room to where it had stood. Gran had left her bonnet on a small table when we went to bed the night before the flood, and when the bonnet was lifted, having floated on the table and quite dry, a tiny mouse sat under it as scared as we were! For a while nobody could explain why we could not find the tea kettle, also the heavy rug from the living room floor. We found it when we tried to light a fire: the action of the water had rolled up the rug as neatly as by hand, and wedged the rug in the chimney. When the rug was pulled out the kettle sat on top of it, quite dry. The living room suite was upholstered green plush and in a week or two, grass was growing fresh and green through the covers.

Whatever my Mother's feelings about the wreckage she did not say much, but just set to and cleared it away. Plenty of help was forthcoming, and we lived upstairs for a while as downstairs didn't dry out very soon. There were twin girls born nearby the night of the flood: doctor and nurse were transported by boat, and soon after the births the wall collapsed and exposed the bedroom to the awful cold of a January morning.

The *Midland Daily Telegraph*, 1 January 1901, reported on the flood:

Nearly all the houses in the low-lying courts of West Orchard had suffered severely, everywhere the same spectacle being visible of wrecked furniture, rooms all reeking wet and slimy, clothing washed away, windows broken, dogs and cats drowned ... One old man named Sherrad ... had to break through a partition into the next house to rescue two children ... Another locality where great distress is prevalent comprises the courts of Spon Street ... which were all under water ...

One poor woman, who supports an octogenarian mother, wordlessly beckoned the relief representatives into her house, and broke down as she showed them the living room. Everything was still dripping wet, and everything that was not broken was spoilt by the water. The grate was cold and damp and the feeble old lady and her miserable cat sat and shivered in the midst of the desolation.

The pitiful sight to be seen in many houses was intensified by the poor and scant efforts at Christmas decoration, little sprigs of holly and mistletoe, and coloured paper bands still hanging on the upper walls, while below the waterline everything was ruined.

An old lady who lives at 4 Spon Street, Mrs Winstanley, and is aged 81 years of age woke up in the night to find her bed afloat in the flood, and was only rescued with difficulty by a neighbour.

Shortly afterwards an inquest was held on a victim of the flood, sixty-four-year-old Joseph Sheward of Hill Street. James McGowran, a neighbour, heard him calling for help and tried to rescue him by throwing a rope to him across the yard and through a broken window through which Sheward was shouting – though he was by then up to his neck in water. Sheward grabbed the rope and McGowran pulled, but could not get him through. Moreover, he actually worried that he might pull off Sheward's arm. Instead, he watched helplessly as the waters advanced. The *Midland Daily Telegraph* reported the tragic scene: 'Witness saw the old man die ---- he thought from the shock and cold, for deceased must have been two hours naked in the water, and he was obliged to let the rope go. Witness had to save his own wife and child.' McGowran also managed to rescue two old ladies, his neighbours, who – as the paper reported – would otherwise surely have drowned.

There were other floods into the twentieth century, but none on this scale. In the 1930s work began on culverting the river to put an end to the risk, and now it can only be seen in four places in the city centre.

ZEPPELINS AND PLANE CRASHES

THE FIRST WORLD War brings many images to the mind, notably the Somme and the horrors of trench warfare – the mud, the death, the terror. Other battlefields were in dry places, such as Gallipoli, where the sun baked the ground so hard that they were unable to bury the dead. My own granddad fought in both these battlegrounds with the Royal Warwickshire Regiment. Coventry's connection to these places is not only the men they supplied, some 35,000 of them, but also the fact that literally thousands of bombs, bullets, planes and tanks which took part in various big pushes were actually made in Coventry. The making of munitions and weapons of war also made Coventry a target for German attacks; it also caused many fatalities amongst those who worked in the trade.

No one would ever imagine that massive grey Zeppelin airships once passed over Coventry with ill-intent. It appears that the first Zeppelin over England appeared in January 1915, bombing King's Lynn and Yarmouth and killing ten people. Coventry thereafter, like many other places,

took its first air-raid precautions. Sirens were set up, shelters dug and the lights were dimmed – Coventry quickly gained the reputation of being the darkest city in England. Anti-aircraft guns were placed outside the Shepherd & Shepherdess, Keresley; in Wyken; at Hearsall Common and Whitley Water Works; and massive searchlights were set up. Two fighter aircraft were allocated to defend the city, based on a temporary airfield in Rugby. The pilots, however, were not keen on the accommodation, and chose to stay at the officers' mess in Castle Bromwich, meaning a 30-mile drive on receiving a warning! Not surprisingly, this particular line of defence proved ineffective.

The first actual appearance of a Zeppelin over Coventry appears to have taken place on 31 January 1916, when the sirens sounded to the sound of a throbbing engine. All the city lights were turned off at the mains and sirens sounded for several minutes. The city was blacked out, and the great grey airship passed over. No bombs were actually dropped, but an eighty-year-old lady living in Brooklyn

A First World War picture showing a Zeppelin under attack. Search lights and guns generally associated with the Second World War were already in use. In this instance, a plane is 'looping the loop' around the L II, brought down on 17 October 1917.

Avenue, Holbrooks, suffered a stroke and died. Her doctor said her demise was brought on by 'shock brought about by the fear of Zeppelins.'

In January of that same year, 1916, Alderman H.B.W. Cresswell visited the Opera House in Hales Street.

I was on leave from the army when *Il Trovatore* was being performed. Suddenly the alarm warning of approaching Zeppelins was given and all the lights were switched off. Some disorder appeared imminent among patrons and the leading man, Cynlais Gibbs, appealed for order and threw in a half-hearted witticism. I replied to him in similar vein, and we indulged in several minutes impromptu cross-talk. The audience laughed then calmed while cycle lamps, etc., were procured to enable the performance to continue. The tenor said he was much obliged to me, but the expected 'Zepps' did not appear.

In the early hours of 13 April 1918, Lieutenant Cecil Noble-Cambell of B Flight, 38 Squadron, based at Buckminster, saw – while patrolling at 16,000ft – a Zeppelin near Birmingham. He closed in on it but was unaware that Lieutenant Brown of C Flight was also advancing on the Zeppelin from the opposite direction. Suddenly the propeller blade of Noble-Cambell's FE2 shattered, forcing him to make a controlled crash in the vicinity of Radford Aerodrome (nearly hitting a wall at White & Poppe's in Whitmore Park). As he clambered out of his fighter it burst into flames. Brown's fighter also took a hit and crashed at the aerodrome. The Zeppelin itself continued quietly chugging across the sky, at the edge of Coventry, totally unaware that it had come under attack. It appears that the two fighters dived blindly on opposite sides of the airship: they probably fired as they swooped down, hitting each other without even knowing it. It has also been suggested that they clipped each other, but this seems less likely. Both men assumed that they had been shot down by the 'Zepp', but it seems that those on board the airship, later

AN EARLY AERIAL DISASTER IN COVENTRY

The 1916 Zeppelin was not the first mysterious object to fly over Coventry. A most unusual death took place in 1910 involving a rather impressive and daring twenty-five-year-old lady called Miss Viola Spencer (Viola Spencer-Kavanagh, to give her full name). On Lillywhite Sports Day, held in Foleshill of that year, Viola was engaged to perform a parachute descent via a balloon. She apparently perched upon a swing, which hung under the parachute – which in turn hung under the balloon. She called out 'goodbye' as the balloon ascended to a great height. Her intention was to release herself over the city and drift down onto the Butts Cricket Ground. However, the balloon slipped the parachute prematurely and Viola floated down in the direction of the Market Hall. There a cross wind hit her, sending her spinning sideways and down. The *Midland Daily Telegraph* later reported the tragic results:

> The large number of spectators were horrified in seeing that the parachute seemed to be descending upon the Market Hall. However in her descent the lady struck on the Centaur Works, West Orchard, catching her feet on the edge of the roof, with the result that the parachute tilted over and both she and it fell with a crash into the roadway, bringing down some telephone wires in the descent. Miss Spencer came to the ground on her face, with sickening force, and was rendered unconscious. Several spectators rushed to the immediate scene of the accident, and raised the fallen lady, who was found to be bleeding profusely from the mouth. A great crowd quickly assembled, [and] West Orchard soon became impassable. A number of policemen also quickly arrived and rendered first aid. The unfortunate parachutist was placed in a motor car and taken to the Coventry and Warwickshire Hospital.

Sadly, this intrepid young lady died five days later. The roof she had fallen onto was some 40ft from the ground. This extraordinary woman wasn't just a balloonist – she had also made a number of flights in aeroplanes, some 300 in total. At the time of the accident she had been practising on a Bleriot and was awaiting a British-built machine to fly the Irish Channel.

---

asked about the day, knew nothing of the event.

The Zeppelin passed over Coventry at 11 p.m. and the lights went out; shortly afterwards the searchlights went into action and the guns opened fire at Keresley, then later from Stubb's Farm, Wyken. While passing over Sowe Common in Walsgrave, the late Reg Johnson recalled:

I remember old Ma Beale tellin' me Snob Thompson used to call in –

they were all Thompsons at the top common. This Zeppelin went over and Snob was out without his trousers and his shirt [shaking his fist at the Zeppelin] and he was saying, 'It's always the same: when you want a policeman you can never find one.' What a policeman was gonna do about it, I don't know!

Bombs were dropped on Baginton Sewerage Farm, a raid that included seven incendiaries which failed to detonate. This was followed by two larger bombs on Whitley Common, one leaving a crater 25ft wide by 8ft deep. Several fighter aircraft were sent to intercept from Radford Aerodrome but they failed to catch up with the airship. One shell fired by anti-aircraft guns at the Zeppelin came down and smashed through the roof at White & Poppe's filling factory, landing 4ft from an explosive magazine. Luckily, it failed to detonate. The casualties of this raid totalled one tree, one cow and two sheep.

The means to bring down these great airships was invented and made in Coventry – namely the incendiary bullet. Twenty-six million of these were made, and it is believed that – with one exception – they were responsible for bringing down all Zeppelins over this country.

The centre of air defence over Coventry was Radford Aerodrome, known as Air Acceptance Park One. This airfield was attached to the Daimler factory, which produced the bi-plane fighter RE8. From here planes were built, collected and flown to airfields around the country, mainly destined for France. The first plane built and flown from here was the single-seater B.E.12, a 'Zeppelin Buster'. On 19 April 1918 Lieutenant Sidney Angus Leith was killed when the RE8 he was testing spun out of control and nosedived from 400ft into the ground over Radford Aerodrome. Three days later Lieutenant A. McDunlop luckily survived a crash when the RE8 he'd collected stalled and spun into the ground. Days later an SE5A crashed at Radford. On the

27 March another RE8 smashed into the ground, killing Lieutenant Harry Laughton; another SE5A crashed in May. The next accident took place on 24 September when a RE8 and a SE5A took off from Radford and collided in mid-air – spinning and locked together, they came down into the ground. Lieutenant Charles Baker, the pilot of the SE5A, escaped alive, but he was seriously injured. Others were not so lucky. The SE5A held two men: one, Airman Welshman, was killed outright, while the other, Lieutenant Berry, later died in hospital.

A witness account exists of this collision: 'At about 10.30 a.m. on the 24th I was standing opposite Mssrs White & Poppe's watchman's lodge and looking up I saw two aeroplanes about five yards apart at a height of 150 feet. They collided and the machines fell on a heap of empty fuse boxes.'

On 1 November 1918 another SE5A stalled, sending Sergeant Austin-Jones plummeting to the ground.

All these crashes – and the fear that a plane might crash into dangerous live munitions causing a massive explosion – meant that concrete bunkers, called 'the dumps', were built at White & Poppe's munitions factory, which lay a short distance north of the airfield. Peter Poppe, of White & Poppe's, wrote: 'The number of machines coming to grief at the back of White and Poppe's and in the Park caused the plans for our further extensions to be modified.'

It was said at the time that some of the crashes coincided with the dinner break at the works – large numbers of young ladies sat outside at this time and watched the dashing pilots, who sometimes put on a show for them.

DANGER BUILDINGS AND CANARY GIRLS

These girls were known locally as 'canary girls', as handling the yellow explosive Tetryl stained their skin yellow. They worked in dangerous conditions, especially those who dealt with detonators (which were notoriously unstable). The bombs that were made here were generally safe until the actual detonators were added. Then they instantly became dangerous – hence the need for the dumps. Remaining munitions continued to be dangerous: White & Poppe, by the war's end, still held a massive stock of bombs waiting to be made safe.

The late Ellen Wilson worked in the 'Danger Building', as it was known. Here detonators were defused. It was dangerous work, but better paid than many other jobs. Her son recalled one of her memories:

There had been one tragedy there: one girl used to carry the tray of deto-nators from the arsenal store over a wooden bridge to the workshop. She was accompanied by a charge hand to unlock the door and relock after she left. One day, as this routine was happening, the girl was returning over the bridge when her sweetheart – who had unexpectedly returned from the war – arrived at the factory gate to meet her. She dropped the tray of detonators in her surprise ... then she tried to pick

the tray up again. She was killed in the explosion, and the charge hand – who was a few paces behind, having locked the door after she left – was injured.

Other types of explosives were also hazardous, such as the drying of fulminate (an explosive used in detonators). This was dried using hot-water pipes, but still constantly exploded; it was recorded that only 12 to 15 tons was ever dried successfully without incident. The plant produced 200,000 black powder pellets a day which were added to the outer case of detonators. These were pressed out by hand until a machine was created to do the job – which worked quite successfully until it too was blown up!

Jeremy Hassell, in his booklet *White & Poppe*, says of the previous incident:

Whether this was the explosion in which a girl died after she had an arm and the side of her face blown off is not known, but a letter written by Mrs Ashmore, a local resident, on 30 March 1917 refers to this, 'There has been a dreadful lot of accidents at White & Poppe lately. Only this morning the magazine caught fire and we all sat here in the office waiting to be blown up. The girls were running down the lane for dear life in their overalls – On Wednesday a girl got her arm and half of her face blown off. She died yesterday.'

There was another girl recorded on a postcard as 'killed in action' here in 1918. By the end of 1916, 4,000 girls and 800 men were working in the filling factory. By the end of the war over 30,000 had worked there; they had filled 30 million fuses and 31 million detonators.

Explosions and fires were a daily hazard in the works. In March 1916 a fire occurred at the factory and Sergeant Henney, a member of the work's fire brigade, entered the detonator workshop, which was filled with choking smoke. The source of this was a lethal bucket full of detonators which was on fire. Henney carried this burning bucket-load down a smoke-filled gantry about 1,000ft long. At the end of this terrifying walk he managed to get outside and dump the bucket into the mud, where he poured water over it – thereby preventing a lethal explosion. Not just a small explosion, either, for a newspaper of the time says: 'an explosion which would undoubtedly have been attended by serious consequences to the factory, and in all probability to the City of Coventry as well.' In other words, Henney risked his life to carry burning detonators through a massive area filled with detonators and explosives which, if they went up, would have had a similar effect to a giant bomb. Henney was awarded the Edward Medal at Buckingham Palace for his bravery, and was afterwards welcomed back to Coventry by thousands of people and then presented with a gold watch inscribed with the words 'a token of admiration from Coventry'.

Coventry's other big ordnance factory was in Red Lane. This consisted of the 'fuse factory' and the naval guns section. Here, as at White & Poppe, many of the workers were women. In the naval section women unusually wore trousers, but in the fuse section they wore dresses. In *Red Lane Reminiscences* (1983), the late Florence Jackson recalled: 'They used to fill the shell bodies with powder, and

Canary girls and young men, probably at the Red Lane ordnance factory. (Colin Walker)

often one blew up ... occasionally you'd get a spark off and it would go ... My stepmother worked there. One of her friends, they said, had her face blown to bits.'

The late Florence Davis recalled another cause of accidents: 'There were two bad accidents there due to someone smoking. I think five were killed, the first time, and two the next.'

The Ordnance Works made many things, including big naval guns up to an 18in diameter. The late Marguerite Thorn of Kenilworth started at the works, at the age of fourteen, in 1916. In 1981 she wrote:

> I used to watch the huge naval guns for HMS Chester, HMS Birkenhead and other warships being turned on massive lathes in the naval shop, which was quarter of a mile long ... Sometimes I watched the guns being loaded on waggons to go by rail across Stoney Stanton Road, through Webster's Brick Works, on past Courtalds and to the main line at Lockhurst Lane. Outside the naval shop near to Swan Lane was an immense cast-iron firing pit for testing the guns before dispatch. When this was in operation it could be heard all over Stoke and Foleshill and further away.

Coventry certainly did its bit during the First World War, with its citizens, permanent or temporary, with 2,587 dying at the Front and, more surprisingly, sometimes back at home too.

GET THE GERMANS

COVENTRY OF 1919 was a slightly strange place. Thousands of soldiers had returned home from the horror of the trenches. Many of these newly demobbed men, many deeply traumatised by their experiences, had no work: in many cases women were still doing their jobs, and to them it must have seemed that the world had turned upside down. Over the country it was the same. As a result of this phenomenon, sporadic riots began to break out, targeting anything that appeared to have German connections.

Even in the early days of the war, it appears, the King's Head Hotel had been threatened with attack because of some unknown German connection. The 19 July was the day that the threats came to fruition, on the day of the Godiva Procession. Pansy Montague rode as the lady, and at first the day went well. Later, however, it began to rain, and the various firework displays which had been planned were cancelled. Angry and disappointed crowds numbering in their hundreds gathered in Broadgate and by 11 p.m. the trouble which was stirring burst

forth when five windows of Messrs Dunn, Coventry's premier hat shop, were smashed. Those looking at the incident through the windows of the King's Head were in for a surprise – they soon became the next target.

Superintendent Langford, then a police constable, was there, and he wrote about the event in 1951:

> I was one of the police officers on duty and we had a tough job to prevent further damage. Truncheons were drawn but we were ordered not to use them. Nonetheless, a section of police in Hertford Street, led by a sergeant, did not hear this order, and they moved forward against the mob ... the crowd turned and fled, with the police chasing them, and the street was soon cleared. In Broadgate the police were reinforced and after a severe struggle were able to force back the crowd. But they had to face a hail of stones, brick-ends and bottles.

The following night crowds again assembled in Broadgate, and soon became threatening. Shop widows started to be indiscriminately smashed, and policemen started to get injured:

Above *The day after the riots in 1919, shops were boarded up in Broadgate and groups of people gather to satisfy their curiosity.*

Right *The corner of Broadgate and Market Street. The shops were boarded to prevent the windows being smashed.*

Every available constable, even the office staff, was called out on duty. Some of the people tore down the planks which were put up to guard shop windows. Women joined the mob, and assisted in the hooliganism. In the Market Square, where building was in progress, granite sets had been placed in a pile. Women had filled their aprons and carried them to the leaders and threw them at anything that was capable of being smashed. Street lamps were the obvious target.

Ironically, most of these stones flying through the air had formed the floor of the site of the old police house in Market Square. The police again dug in, fighting running street battles without truncheons and dragging people off, and eventually, by 2 a.m., the streets were clear.

The next night the unrest began again: between 10 p.m. and 11 p.m. more windows were smashed. Superintendent Langford reported his memories of that evening, as the mood of the crowd darkened:

I was struck twice with heavy stones. Then looting began. At last someone gave the order to draw truncheons and we used them to beat off the hooligans. It was impossible, however, to find the ringleaders, and many innocent

About half of Coventry's police force posing outside the Guildhall in around 1919. (Coventry Police Museum)

people suffered. We charged down Cross Cheaping in battle array and the rioters fled before us into Bishop Street, Hales Street and Well Street. With some of my colleagues we turned into Stoney Stanton Road, where the mob fought a fierce rearguard action, tearing up stones forming the border of the flower beds and throwing them at us. About 100 people were treated in hospital that night. Some of them were stretcher cases, but there was nothing more serious than broken arms or ribs.

On returning to the police station we found a bus load of police reinforcements from Birmingham, but with a touch of pride we were able to tell them: 'We used our tools and finished the job.'

This was the last large-scale riot ever to take place in Coventry's 'Bloody' history.